THE ANNOTATED LUTHER STUDY EDITION

The Babylonian Captivity
of the Church

1520

THE ANNOTATED LUTHER STUDY EDITION

The Babylonian Captivity of the Church

1520

ERIK H. HERRMANN

Paul W. Robinson
EDITOR

Fortress Press
Minneapolis

The Babylonian Captivity of the Church, 1520
THE ANNOTATED LUTHER STUDY EDITION

Unless otherwise noted, Scripture quotations are from New Revised Standard Version Bible, copyright © 1989 by the Division of Education of the National Council of Churches of Christ in the United States of America.

Excerpted from The Annotated Luther, Volume 3, *Church and Sacaraments* (Minneapolis: Fortress Press, 2016), Paul W. Robinson, volume editor.

Fortress Press Publication Staff:
Scott Tunseth, Project Editor
Alicia Ehlers, Production Manager
Laurie Ingram, Cover Design
Esther Diley, Permissions

Copyeditor: David Lott
Series design and typesetting: Ann Delgehausen, Trio Bookworks
Proofreader: Paul Kobelski, HK Scriptorium

Library of Congress Cataloging-in-Publication Data is available

Print ISBN: 978-1-5064-1347-1
eISBN: 978-1-5064-1348-8

The paper used in this publication meets the minimum requirements of American National Standard for Information Sciences—Permanence of Paper for Printed Library Materials, ANSI Z329, 48-1984.

Manufactured in the U.S.A.

Contents

Publisher's Note

About the Annotated Luther Study Edition

The volumes in the Annotated Luther Study Edition series have first been published in one of the comprehensive volumes of The Annotated Luther series. A description of that series and the volumes can be found in the Series Introduction (p. vii). While each comprehensive Annotated Luther volume can easily be used in classroom settings, we also recognize that treatises are often assigned individually for reading and study. To facilitate classroom and group use, we have pulled key treatises along with their introductions, annotations, and images directly from the Annotated Luther Series volumes.

Please note that the study edition page numbers match the page numbers of the larger Annotated Luther volume in which it first appeared. We have intentionally retained the same page numbering to facilitate use of the study editions and larger volumes side by side.

The Babylonian Captivity of the Church, 1520,
was first published in The Annotated Luther series,
volume 3, *Church and Sacraments* (2016).

Series Introduction

Engaging the Essential Luther

Even after five hundred years Martin Luther continues to engage and challenge each new generation of scholars and believers alike. With 2017 marking the five-hundredth anniversary of Luther's *95 Theses*, Luther's theology and legacy are being explored around the world with new questions and methods and by diverse voices. His thought invites ongoing examination, his writings are a staple in classrooms and pulpits, and he speaks to an expanding assortment of conversation partners who use different languages and hale from different geographical and social contexts.

The six volumes of The Annotated Luther edition offer a flexible tool for the global reader of Luther, making many of his most important writings available in the *lingua franca* of our times as one way of facilitating interest in the Wittenberg reformer. They feature new introductions, annotations, revised translations, and textual notes, as well as visual enhancements (illustrations, art, photos, maps, and timelines). The Annotated Luther edition embodies Luther's own cherished principles of communication. Theological writing, like preaching, needs to reflect human beings' lived experience, benefits from up-to-date scholarship, and should be easily accessible to all. These volumes are designed to help teachers and students, pastors and laypersons, and other professionals in ministry understand the context in which the documents were written, recognize how the documents have shaped Protestant and Lutheran thinking, and interpret the meaning of these documents for faith and life today.

The Rationale for This Edition

For any reader of Luther, the sheer number of his works presents a challenge. Well over one hundred volumes comprise the scholarly edition of Luther's works, the so-called Weimar Ausgabe (WA), a publishing enterprise begun in 1883 and only completed in the twenty-first century. From 1955 to 1986, fifty-five volumes came to make up *Luther's Works* (American Edition) (LW), to which Concordia Publishing House, St. Louis, is adding still more. This English-language contribution to Luther studies, matched by similar translation projects for Erasmus of Rotterdam and John Calvin, provides a theological and historical gold mine for those interested in studying Luther's thought. But even these volumes are not always easy to use and are hardly portable. Electronic forms have increased availability, but preserving Luther in book form and providing readers with manageable selections are also important goals.

Moreover, since the publication of the WA and the first fifty-five volumes of the LW, research on the Reformation in general and on Martin Luther in particular has broken new ground and evolved, as has knowledge regarding the languages in which Luther wrote. Up-to-date information from a variety of sources is brought together in The Annotated Luther, building on the work done by previous generations of scholars. The language and phrasing of the translations have also been updated to reflect modern English usage. While the WA and, in a derivative way, LW remain the central source for Luther scholarship, the present critical and annotated English translation facilitates research internationally and invites a new generation of readers for whom Latin and German might prove an unsurpassable obstacle to accessing Luther. The WA provides the basic Luther texts (with some exceptions); the LW provides the basis for almost all translations.

Defining the "Essential Luther"

Deciding which works to include in this collection was not easy. Criteria included giving attention to Luther's initial key works; considering which publications had the most impact in his day and later; and taking account of Luther's own favorites, texts addressing specific issues of continued importance for today, and Luther's exegetical works. Taken as a whole, these works present the many sides of Luther, as reformer, pastor, biblical interpreter, and theologian. To serve today's readers and by using categories similar to those found in volumes 31–47 of Luther's works (published by Fortress Press), the volumes offer in the main a thematic rather than strictly chronological approach to Luther's writings. The volumes in the series include:

> Volume 1: *The Roots of Reform* (Timothy J. Wengert, editor)
> Volume 2: *Word and Faith* (Kirsi I. Stjerna, editor)
> Volume 3: *Church and Sacraments* (Paul W. Robinson, editor)
> Volume 4: *Pastoral Writings* (Mary Jane Haemig, editor)
> Volume 5: *Christian Life in the World* (Hans J. Hillerbrand, editor)
> Volume 6: *The Interpretation of Scripture* (Euan K. Cameron, editor)

The History of the Project

In 2011 Fortress Press convened an advisory board to explore the promise and parameters of a new English edition of Luther's essential works. Board members Denis Janz, Robert Kolb, Peter Matheson, Christine Helmer, and Kirsi Stjerna deliberated with

Fortress Press publisher Will Bergkamp to develop a concept and identify contributors. After a review with scholars in the field, college and seminary professors, and pastors, it was concluded that a single-language edition was more desirable than dual-language volumes.

In August 2012, Hans Hillerbrand, Kirsi Stjerna, and Timothy Wengert were appointed as general editors of the series with Scott Tunseth from Fortress Press as the project editor. The general editors were tasked with determining the contents of the volumes and developing the working principles of the series. They also helped with the identification and recruitment of additional volume editors, who in turn worked with the general editors to identify volume contributors. Mastery of the languages and unique knowledge of the subject matter were key factors in identifying contributors. Most contributors are North American scholars and native English speakers, but The Annotated Luther includes among its contributors a circle of international scholars. Likewise, the series is offered for a global network of teachers and students in seminary, university, and college classes, as well as pastors, lay teachers, and adult students in congregations seeking background and depth in Lutheran theology, biblical interpretation, and Reformation history.

Editorial Principles

The volume editors and contributors have, with few exceptions, used the translations of LW as the basis of their work, retranslating from the WA for the sake of clarity and contemporary usage. Where the LW translations have been substantively altered, explanatory notes have often been provided. More importantly, contributors have provided marginal notes to help readers understand theological and historical references. Introductions have been expanded and sharpened to reflect the very latest historical and theological research. In citing the Bible, care has been taken to reflect the German and Latin texts commonly used in the sixteenth century rather than modern editions, which often employ textual sources that were unavailable to Luther and his contemporaries.

Finally, all pieces in The Annotated Luther have been revised in the light of modern principles of inclusive language. This is not always an easy task with a historical author, but an intentional effort has been made to revise language throughout, with creativity and editorial liberties, to allow Luther's theology to speak free from unnecessary and unintended gender-exclusive language. This important principle provides an opportunity to translate accurately certain gender-neutral German and Latin expressions that Luther employed—for example, the Latin word *homo* and the German *Mensch* mean "human being," not simply "males." Using the words *man* and *men* to translate such terms would create an ambiguity not present in the original texts. The focus is on linguistic accuracy and Luther's intent. Regarding creedal formulations and trinitarian language, Luther's own expressions have been preserved, without entering the complex and important contemporary debates over language for God and the Trinity.

The 2017 anniversary of the publication of the *95 Theses* is providing an opportunity to assess the substance of Luther's role and influence in the Protestant Reformation. Revisiting Luther's essential writings not only allows reassessment of Luther's rationale and goals but also provides a new look at what Martin Luther was about and why new generations would still wish to engage him. We hope these six volumes offer a compelling invitation.

Hans J. Hillerbrand
Kirsi I. Stjerna
Timothy J. Wengert
General Editors

Abbreviations

ANF	Ante-Nicene Fathers
ASD	*Desiderii Erasmi Roterodami Opera omnia* (Amsterdam: North Holland, 1969–)
BC	*The Book of Concord*, ed. Robert Kolb and Timothy J. Wengert (Minneapolis: Fortress Press, 2000)
BCorr	*Correspondance de Martin Bucer*, Martini Buceri Opera omnia. Series 3, ed. Jean Rott et al. (Leiden: Brill, 1979–)
BDS	*Martin Bucers Deutsche Schriften*, Opera omnia. Series 1, ed. Robert Stupperich et al. (Gütersloh: Gütersloher Verlagshaus G. Mohn, 1960–)
CA	*The Augsburg Confession*
CCSL	*Corpus Christianorum Series Latina*
CH	*The Church History of Rufinus of Aquileia: Books 10 and 11*, trans. Philip R. Amidon (New York: Oxford University Press, 1997)
CIC	*Corpus Iuris Canonici*, ed. Emil Louis Richter and Emil Friedberg, 2 vols. (Graz: Akademische Druck- u. Verlagsanstalt, 1959)
CR	*Corpus Reformatorum*
CSEL	*Corpus Scriptorum Ecclesiasticorum Latinorum*
DRTA. JR	*Deutsche Reichstagsakten unter Kaiser Karl V*, ed. Historische Kommission bei der Bayerischen Akademie der Wissenschaften (Gotha, 1893–).
ELW	*Evangelical Lutheran Worship* (Minneapolis: Augsburg Fortress, 2006).
GCS	*Die Griechischen Christlichen Schriftsteller der Ersten drei Jahrhunderte* (Berlin: Akademie Verlag, 1897–)
HZW	*Huldrych Zwingli: Writings*, ed. E. J. Furcha and H. Wayne Pipkin, 2 vols. (Allison Park, PA: Pickwick Publications, 1984)
LC	*The Large Catechism*
LSB	*Lutheran Service Book* (St. Louis: Concordia, 2006)
LW	*Luther's Works* [American edition], ed. Helmut Lehmann and Jaroslav Pelikan, 55 vols. (Philadelphia: Fortress Press/St. Louis: Concordia, 1955–1986).
LWZ	*The Latin Works and Correspondence of Huldreich Zwingli*, ed. Samuel Macauley Jackson, 3 vols. (New York, 1912; Philadelphia, 1922, 1929)
MLStA	*Martin Luther: Studienausgabe*, ed. Hans-Ulrich Delius, 6 vols (Berlin & Leipzig: Evangelische Verlagsanstalt, 1979–1999)
MPG	*Patrologiae cursus completus, series graeca* ed. Jacques-Paul Migne, 166 vols. (Paris, 1857–1866)
MPL	*Patrologiae cursus completus, series latina*, ed. Jacques-Paul Migne, 217 vols. (Paris, 1844–64)
NPNF	*Nicene and Post-Nicene Fathers*, ed. Philip Schaaf and Henry Wace, series 1 [NPNF1], 14 vols.; and series 2 [NPNF2], 14 vols. (London: T&T Clark, 1886–1900)

ODCC	*The Oxford Dictionary of the Christian Church*, ed. F. L. Cross, 3d rev. ed., ed. E. A. Livingstone (Oxford: Oxford University Press, 2005)
OER	*Oxford Encyclopedia of the Reformation*, ed. Hans J. Hillerbrand, 4 vols. (New York: Oxford University Press, 1996)
STh	Thomas Aquinas, *Summa Theologica*
TAL	The Annotated Luther
W²	*Dr. Martin Luthers sämmtliche Schriften*, ed. Johann Georg Walch, 23 vols. (St. Louis: Concordia, 1881–1910)
WA	*Luthers Werke: Kritische Gesamtausgabe [Schriften]*, 73 vols. (Weimar: H. Böhlau, 1883–2009)
WA DB	*Luthers Werke: Kritische Gesamtausgabe: Deutsche Bibel*, 12 vols. (Weimar: H. Böhlau, 1906–1961)
WA Br	*Luthers Werke: Kritische Gesamtausgabe: Briefwechsel*, 18 vols. (Weimar: H. Böhlau, 1930–1985)
WA TR	*Luthers Werke: Kritische Gesamtausgabe: Tischreden*, 6 vols. (Weimar: H. Böhlau, 1912–1921)
Wander	*Deutsches Sprichwörter-Lexikon*, ed. K. F. Wander, 5 vols. (Darmstadt: Wissenschaftliche Buchgesellschaft, 1964)
WPBW	*Willibald Pirckheimers Briefwechsel*, ed. Emil Reicke et al., 7 vols. (Munich: Beck, 1940–2009)
Z	*Huldreich Zwinglis sämtliche Werke*, ed. Emil Egli et al., Corpus Reformatorum 88–108 (Leipzig/Zurich: Heinsius/TVZ, 1905–2013)

The Babylonian Captivity of the Church

1520

ERIK H. HERRMANN

INTRODUCTION

At the end of his German treatise *Address to the Christian Nobil-ity* (*An den christlichen Adel deutscher Nation*), Luther dropped a hint of what was coming next: "I know another little song about Rome and the Romanists. If their ears are itching to hear it, I will sing that one to them, too—and pitch it in the highest key!" This "little song" Luther would call a "prelude" on the captivity of the Roman church—or the *Babylonian Captivity of the Church*, published just a few months later in October of 1520. A polemi-cal treatise, it was truly "pitched high," with Luther hiding little of his dissatisfaction with the prevalent sacramental practices sanctioned by Rome. Although he fully expected the work to elicit a cacophony of criticisms from his opponents, Luther's positive aim was to set forth a reconsideration of the sacramen-tal Christian life that centered on the Word. His thesis is that the papacy had distorted the sacraments with its own traditions and regulations, transforming them into a system of control and coercion. The evangelical liberty of the sacramental promises had been replaced by a papal absolutism that, like a feudal lord-ship, claimed its own jurisdictional liberties and privileges over the totality of Christian life through a sacramental system that spanned birth to death. Yet Luther does not replace one tyranny

1. *Anfechtung(en)* embraces several concepts and is not readily translated into a single English word. It can be simply understood as "temptation" or "trial" (Lat. *tentatio*) and is employed in this manner by Luther in his German translation of the Bible. But even these examples do not give a single picture on the nature of the temptation and from whence it comes. In some places *Anfechtung* is a struggle within—a conflict with flesh and spirit (e.g., Matt. 26:41); in other places the trial seems to come from the outside—from enemies and persecuters of the church (Luke 8:13 and James 1:12). In Luther's writings, he adds to the complexity of the term as he reflects both upon his own personal experiences of *Anfechtung* and the theological implications attached to them. At the basic level, they are experienced as a contradiction of God's love and protection, a perceived antagonism and hostility to the security of one's salvation. Satan's accusations, self-doubt and the weakness of the flesh, and God's wrath are all various aspects of this experience. Yet for Luther, such trials are ultimately to be received as a blessing from God, a tool of his fatherly love to refine faith and strengthen one's confidence in God's Word and promises. Thus, he describes *Anfechtung* as one of the necessary experiences for the making of a Christian theologian: "This is the touchstone which teaches you not only to know and understand, but also to experience how right, how true, how sweet, how lovely, how mighty, how comforting God's Word is, wisdom beyond all wisdom" (*Preface to the Wittenberg Edition of Luther's German Writings*, TAL 4).

for another; his argument for a return to the biblical understanding of the sacraments is moderated by a consideration of traditions and external practices in relation to their effects on the individual conscience and faith.

On the one hand, Luther's treatise is shaped by some of the specific arguments of his opponents. There are two treatises in particular to which Luther reacts. The first is by an Italian Dominican, Isidoro Isolani (c. 1480–1528), who wrote a tract calling for Luther's recantation, *Revocatio Martini Lutheri Augustiniani ad sanctam sedem* (1519). The second writing, appearing in July of 1520, was by the Leipzig theologian Augustinus Alveld (c. 1480–1535), who argued against Luther on the topic of communion in "both kinds." In some sense, the *Babylonian Captivity* serves as Luther's reply.

But Luther's ideas on the sacraments had been in development for some time before. His early personal struggles with penance and the Mass are well known and were the context for much of his *Anfechtungen*[1] and spiritual trials in the monastery. Likewise, his subsequent clarity on the teaching of justification and faith quickly reshaped his thinking on the sacramental life. By 1519, he had decided that only three of the seven sacraments could be defined as such on the basis of Scripture, publishing a series of sermons that year on the sacraments of penance, baptism, and the Lord's Supper.[a] In 1520, he wrote another, more extensive treatise on the Lord's Supper, a *Treatise on the New Testament*. In all of these works, the sacrament chiefly consists in the divine promise and the faith which grasps it. So it is in the *Babylonian Captivity*, where the correlative of faith and promise is the *leitmotif* that runs through the entire work.

As Luther discusses each of the sacraments, he exhibits a remarkable combination of detailed, penetrating biblical interpretation and pastoral sensitivity for the common person. In fact, it is precisely the perceived lack of attention to Scripture and to pastoral care that drives Luther's ire and polemic. Christians are being fleeced, coerced, and misled by those who should be guiding and caring for consciences. The errors of Rome are

---

a   *The Sacrament of Penance* (LW 35:9–23; WA 2:714–23); *The Holy and Blessed Sacrament of Baptism* (LW 35:29–45; WA 2:727–37); *The Blessed Sacrament of the Holy and True Body of Christ and the Brotherhoods* (LW 35:49–73; WA 2:742–58). All are included in TAL 1.

intolerable because they are so injurious to faith. The most egregious for Luther was how the Eucharist was understood and practiced. Here he identifies three "captivities" of the Mass by which the papacy imprisons the Christian church: the reservation of the cup, the doctrine of transubstantiation, and the use of the Mass as a sacrifice and work to gain divine favor. In all three of these areas, Luther focuses on the pastoral implications of Rome's misuse and tyranny.

The *Babylonian Captivity* is written in Latin, attesting to the technical nature of the topic and to the education of Luther's audience. It is clear that he assumes for his reader at least a broad knowledge of Scholastic theology and, for his humanist readership, a facility with classical allusions which, relative to Luther's other writings, are not infrequent. The reception of the work was a mixed one. Georg Spalatin (1484-1545), the elector's secretary,[2] was worried about the effects the tone would have. Erasmus[3] believed (perhaps rightly) that the breach was now irreparable. Johannes Bugenhagen (1485-1558) was appalled upon his first reading, but upon closer study became convinced that Luther was in the right, and soon became Luther's trusted colleague, co-reformer, and friend. Henry VIII of England (1491-1547) even entered into the fray, writing his own refutation of Luther, a *Defense of the Seven Sacraments*, for which he received the title *Fidei defensor* from the pope. The papal bull[4] threatening Luther with excommunication was already on its way, so in some sense Luther hardly felt he could make matters worse. But in the end, the *Babylonian Captivity* had the effect of galvanizing both opponents and supporters. It became the central work for which Luther had to answer at the Diet of Worms in 1521.

Some of Luther's expressed positions—though provocative at the time—became less agreeable to his followers later on. In particular, Luther seemed ambivalent regarding the role of laws in civil affairs, suggesting that the gospel was a better guide for rulers. Luther himself deemed this position deficient when faced with the Peasants' War in 1525. Likewise, when discussing marriage, Luther was inclined to dismiss the manifold laws and regulations that had grown around the institution and rely only on biblical mandates and examples. This led to some of his more controversial remarks regarding the permissibility of bigamy. After the marital scandal of Philip of Hesse,[5] which ensued in part from following Luther's advice, these remarks were deemed

2. Spalatin served Elector Frederick III the Wise (b. 1463) from 1509 till Frederick's death in 1525.

3. Erasmus of Rotterdam (1466-1536) was a Dutch humanist whose works in moral philosophy and editions of the church fathers and the Greek New Testament made him famous throughout Europe.

4. Pope Leo X (1475-1521) issued the papal bull *Exsurge domine* calling for Luther's excommunication in 1520.

5. Philip I, landgrave of Hesse (1504-1567), was a supporter of the Reformation and used his political authority to encourage Protestantism in Hesse. Soon after he married Christine of Saxony in 1523, he engaged in an adulterous affair, and by 1526 was considering how to make bigamy permissible. Luther counseled Philip against this, advising Christians to avoid bigamous marriage, except in extreme circumstances.

A portrait of Philip I, Landgrave of Hesse, and his wife
Christine of Saxony, painted by Jost V. Hoff.

unacceptable. When Luther's works were first collected and published in Jena and Wittenberg, the publishers excised these portions from Luther's treatise. These sections are indicated in the annotations of this edition.

THE BABYLONIAN CAPTIVITY OF THE CHURCH[6]

A PRELUDE OF MARTIN LUTHER ON THE BABYLONIAN CAPTIVITY OF THE CHURCH

Jesus

MARTIN LUTHER, AUGUSTINIAN, to his friend, Hermann Tulich,[7] greeting.

Whether I wish it or not, I am compelled to become more learned every day, with so many and such able masters eagerly driving me on and making me work. Some two years ago I wrote on indulgences, but in such a way that I now deeply regret having published that little book.[8] At that time I still clung with a mighty superstition to the tyranny of Rome, and so I held that indulgences should not be altogether rejected, seeing that they were approved by the common consent of so many. No wonder, for at the time it was only I rolling this boulder by myself.[9] Afterwards, thanks to Sylvester,[10] and aided by those friars who so strenuously defended indulgences, I saw that they were nothing but impostures of the Roman flatterers, by which they rob people of their money and their faith in God. Would that I could prevail upon the booksellers and persuade all who have read them to burn the whole of my booklets on indulgences,[b] and instead of all that I have written on this subject adopt this proposition: INDULGENCES ARE WICKED DEVICES OF THE FLATTERERS OF ROME.

---

b   In addition to the *Ninety-Five Theses*, WA 1:233–38; LW 31:17–33; TAL 1:13–46, these include: *Explanations of the Ninety-Five Theses*, WA 1:525–628; *A Sermon on Indulgences and Grace*, WA 1:243–56; *The Freedom of the "Sermon on Papal Indulgences and Grace" of Doctor Martin Luther against the "Refutation," Being Completely Fabricated to Insult That Very Sermon*, WA 1:380–93.

6. The English translation for this edition is a revision of that which is found in vol. 36 of *Luther's Works* (Philadelphia: Muhlenberg Press, 1959), 3–126. The revisions are based on WA 6:497–573, and *Martin Luther: Studien Ausgabe*, vol. 2 (Leipzig: Evangelische Verlagsanstalt, 1982), 168–259. Annotations and footnotes are the work of the editors but are also informed by notes included in previous critical editions.

7. Hermann Tulich was born at Steinheim (c. 1488), near Paderborn, in Westphalia. He studied in Wittenberg in 1508 and in 1512 matriculated at the University of Leipzig where he was a proofreader in Melchior Lotter's printing house. He returned to Wittenberg in 1519 and received the doctorate in 1520 and became professor of poetry. He was a devoted supporter of Luther. Eventually he became rector of the Johanneum gymnasium at Lüneberg from 1532 until his death on 28 July 1540.

8. Luther apparently is referring to the *Explanations of the Ninety-Five Theses* (1518), WA 1:522f.; LW 31:83–252; but compare also *A Sermon on Indulgences and Grace* (1518), WA 1:243–56, written around the same time. There he noted that indulgences were not necessary, yet he deemed them permissible for "lazy Christians." See also TAL 1:57–66.

9. A reference to the Greek myth of Sisyphus rather than, as some have suggested, to the proverb from Erasmus's *Adagia* (2, 4, 40): *Saxum volutum non obducitur musco*—"a rolling stone gathers no moss."

10. Sylvester Prierias (i.e., Mazzolini), from Prierio in Piedmont (1456–1523), was a Dominican prior. As an official court theologian for Pope Leo X (*magistri sacri palati*, "Master of the Sacred Palace"), Prierias was ordered to provide theological critique of Luther's *Ninety-Five Theses*. In 1518, Prierias wrote his *Dialogus de potestate papae* ("Dialogue on the Power of the Pope"), which set out a general critique of Luther's arguments against the theology behind indulgences. Like Luther's other opponents (the Dominicans Johann Tetzel [1475–1521] and Jacob van Hoogstraaten (c. 1460–1527), as well as Johann Eck), Prierias shifted the debate toward church authority rather than focusing solely on the question of indulgences.

11. Johann Eck (born Maier; 1486–1543), from the Swabian village of Eck, became professor at Ingolstadt in Bavaria in 1510. His opposition to Luther began with his criticism of the *Ninety-Five Theses* in his *Obelisci*, which led to heated exchanges with Luther and his colleague Andreas Bodenstein von Karlstadt (1486–1541) and culminated with the Leipzig Disputation in 1519. Hieronymus Emser (1477–1527), the secretary and chaplain of Duke George of Saxony (1471–1539), had been a humanist professor at Erfurt in the days that Luther attended. Emser published several works against Luther after the Leipzig debate. See David V. N. Bagchi, *Luther's Earliest Opponents: Catholic Controversialists, 1518–1525* (Minneapolis: Fortress Press, 1991).

12. Only a few months before, Luther expressed this opinion in his treatise *On the Papacy in Rome against the Most Celebrated Romanist in Leipzig*, LW 39:49–104. Cf. *Resolutio Lutheriana super propositione sua decima tertia de potestate papae* (1519), WA 2:180–240.

Next, Eck and Emser and their fellow conspirators undertook to instruct me concerning the primacy of the pope.[11] Here too, not to prove ungrateful to such learned men, I acknowledge that I have profited much from their labors. For while I denied the divine authority of the papacy, I still admitted its human authority.[12] But after hearing and reading the super-subtle

Johann Eck (1486–1543)

subtleties of these showoffs,[c] with which they so adroitly prop up their idol (for my mind is not altogether unteachable in these matters), I now know for certain that the papacy is the kingdom of Babylon and the power of Nimrod, the mighty hunter.[13] Once more, therefore, that all may turn out to my friends' advantage, I beg both the booksellers and my readers that after burning what I have published on this subject they hold to this proposition: THE PAPACY IS THE MIGHTY HUNT OF THE BISHOP OF ROME. This is proved by the arguments of Eck, Emser, and the Leipzig lecturer on the Scriptures.[14]

[Communion in Both Kinds]

Now they are making a game of schooling me concerning communion in both kinds[15] and other weighty subjects: this is the task[d] lest I listen in vain to these self-serving teachers of mine.[16] A certain Italian friar of Cremona has written a "Recantation of Martin Luther before the Holy See," which is not that I revoke anything, as the words declare, but that he revokes me.[17] This is

13. A reference to Gen. 10:8-9: "Cush fathered Nimrod; he was the first on earth to be a mighty man. He was a mighty hunter before the LORD. Therefore it is said, 'Like Nimrod a mighty hunter before the LORD.'" Luther here voices the criticism that the pope was seeking power rather than being a good pastor. So he describes the pope as a "mighty hunter" and his use of authority as a "mighty hunt" rather than describing him as a shepherd tending the sheep.

14. Augustinus Alveld was a Franciscan professor at Leipzig who wrote a treatise against Luther in April of 1520, *Concerning the Apostolic See, Whether It Is a Divine Law or Not*, which sparked Luther's response *On the Papacy in Rome* (see n.8 above).

15. In June 1520, Alveld wrote a treatise against Luther on communion in both kinds, *Tractatus de communione sub utraque specie.* Luther already proposed restoring the cup to the laity in two earlier treatises: *The Blessed Sacrament of the Holy and True Body of Christ, and the Brotherhoods* (1519), LW 35:50; TAL 1:225–56; and *Treatise on the New Testament, That Is, the Holy Mass* (1520), LW 35:106–7.

16. The original Latin here is *Cratippos meos*, a reference to Cratippus of Pergamon (first century BCE), a philosopher who taught in Athens. Because he was an instructor of Cicero's son, Cratippus gained the famed orator's favor, thereby gaining Roman citizenship. The reference is consistent with Luther's opinion of his opponents as flatterers and sycophants.

17. Isidoro Isolani, a Dominican from Milan, published *Revocatio Martini Lutheri Augustiniani ad sanctam sedem* on 22 November 1519 in Cremona.

c   The original Latin here is *Trossulorum*, a reference to Roman knights who conquered the city of Trossulum in Etruria (central Italy) without the aid of foot soldiers (*Pliny* 32, 2; *Seneca*, ep. 87). Later the term was used in a derogatory sense of a conceited dandy.

d   This phrase is perhaps a reference to Virgil's *Aeneid* 6, 129: ". . . *Hoc opus, hic labor est*" ("that is the work, that is the task"), wherein the Sibyl warns Aeneas that his desire to enter Hades is simple; it is *leaving* hell that is the difficult task.

18. A barb that would certainly delight his humanist readers.

19. Tomasso de Vio (Cardinal) Cajetan (1469–1534), vicar general of the Dominican order and influential Aquinas scholar, interviewed Luther at Augsburg in 1518 as papal legate in order to acquire a recantation. His three-day debate with Luther on indulgences, Aquinas, canon law, and church authority was recounted and critically reviewed by Luther in his published *Proceedings at Augsburg* (1518), LW 31:253–92; TAL 1:121–66.

20. Luther's response to Sylvester Prierias, *Ad dialogum Silvestri Prieratis de potestate papae responsio*, was published in 1518.

21. The title page of Alveld's treatise contained twenty-six lines. The "clogs" (*calopodia* = *calcipodium*) that Luther mentioned were the wooden-soled sandals worn by the Observant Franciscans.

22. Luther is referring to the unusual spelling, IHSVH, for Jesus that Alveld tries to justify by arguments which involve an admixture of the three languages.

23. Alveld belonged to the stricter part of the Franciscan order, known as the Observantines. Luther is playing on this word.

the kind of Latin the Italians are beginning to write nowadays.[18] Another friar, a German of Leipzig, that same lecturer, as you know, on the whole canon of Scripture[e] has written against me concerning the sacrament in both kinds and is about to perform, as I understand, still greater and more marvelous things. The Italian[f] was canny enough to conceal his name, fearing perhaps the fate of Cajetan[19] and Sylvester.[20] The man of Leipzig, on the other hand, as becomes a fierce and vigorous German, boasts on his ample title page of his name, his life, his sanctity, his learning, his office, his fame, his honor, almost his very clogs.[21] From him I shall doubtless learn a great deal, since he writes his dedicatory epistle to the Son of God himself: so familiar are these saints with Christ who reigns in heaven! Here it seems three magpies are addressing me, the first in good Latin, the second in better Greek, the third in the best Hebrew.[22] What do you think, my dear Hermann, I should do, but prick up my ears?[g] The matter is being dealt with at Leipzig by the "Observance" of the Holy Cross.[23]

Cajetan (at the table, far left) and Luther (standing right) at Augsburg. Colored woodcut from Ludwig Rabus, *Historien der Heyligen Ausserwählten Gottes Zeugen* (Straßburg, 1557).

e   I.e., Alveld.

f   I.e., Isolani.

Fool that I was, I had hitherto thought that it would be a good thing if a general council were to decide that the sacrament should be administered to the laity in both kinds.[h] This view our more-than-learned friar would correct, declaring that neither Christ nor the apostles had either commanded or advised that both kinds be administered to the laity; it was therefore left to the judgment of the church what to do or not to do in this matter, and the church must be obeyed. These are his words.

You will perhaps ask, what madness has entered into the man, or against whom is he writing? For I have not condemned the use of one kind, but have left the decision about the use of both kinds to the judgment of the church. This is the very thing he attempts to assert, in order to attack me with this same argument. My answer is that this sort of argument is common to all who write against Luther: either they assert the very things they assail, or they set up a man of straw whom they may attack. This is the way of Sylvester and Eck and Emser, and of the men of Cologne and Louvain,[24] and if this friar had not been one of their kind, he would never have written against Luther.

This man turned out to be more fortunate than his fellows, however, for in his effort to prove that the use of both kinds was neither commanded nor advised, but left to the judgment of the church, he brings forward the Scriptures to prove that the use of one kind for the laity was ordained by the command of Christ.[i] So it is true, according to this new interpreter of the Scriptures, that the use of one kind was not commanded and at the same time was commanded by Christ! This novel kind of argument is, as you know, the one which these dialecticians[25] of Leipzig are especially fond of using. Does not Emser profess to speak fairly of me in his earlier book,[26] and then, after I had convicted him of the foulest envy and shameful lies, confess, when about to confute me in his later book,[j] that both were true, and that he has written in both a friendly and an unfriendly spirit? A fine fellow, indeed, as you know!

24. In February of 1520, the theological faculties of Louvain and Cologne published a condemnation of Luther's doctrine based on his collected Latin writings as printed by the Basel printer Johann Froben in 1518.

25. A name derived from the discipline of dialectic, or logic, which was one of the three basic disciplines of medieval education, along with grammar and rhetoric.

26. Emser first published a report of the Leipzig debate between Luther and Eck with his interpretation of it, *De disputatione Lipsicensi, quantum ad Boemos obiter deflexa est* (1519).

g   *"Aures arrigam,"* a common classical turn of phrase, cf. Terence, *Andria* 5, 4, 30; Virgil, *Aeneid* 1, 152; Erasmus, *Adagia* 3, 2, 56.

h   See *The Blessed Sacrament of the Holy and True Body of Christ, and the Brotherhoods* (1519), LW 35:45–74; TAL 1:225–56. Cf. *Treatise on the New Testament, That Is, the Holy Mass* (1520), LW 35:106–7.

i   See below where Luther details Alveld's interpretation of John 6.

j   *A venatione Luteriana aegocerotis assertio* (1519).

But listen to our distinguished distinguisher of "kinds," to whom the decision of the church and the command of Christ are the same thing, and again the command of Christ and no command of Christ are the same thing. With such dexterity he proves that only one kind should be given to the laity, by the command of Christ, that is, by the decision of the church. He puts it in capital letters, thus: THE INFALLIBLE FOUNDATION. Then he treats John 6[:35, 41] with incredible wisdom, where Christ speaks of the bread of heaven and the bread of life, which is he himself. The most learned fellow not only refers these words to the Sacrament of the Altar, but because Christ says: "I am the living bread" [John 6:51] and not "I am the living cup," he actually concludes that we have in this passage the institution of the sacrament in only one kind for the laity. But here follow the words: "For my flesh is food indeed, and my blood is drink indeed" [John 6:55] and, "Unless you eat the flesh of the Son of Man and drink his blood" [John 6:53]. When it dawned upon the good friar that these words speak undeniably for both kinds and against one kind—presto! how happily and learnedly he slips out of the quandary by asserting that in these words Christ means to say only that whoever receives the sacrament in one kind receives therein both flesh and blood. This he lays down as his "infallible foundation" of a structure so worthy of the holy and heavenly "Observance."

I pray you now to learn along with me from this that in John 6 Christ commands the administration of the sacrament in one kind, yet in such a way that his commanding means leaving it to the decision of the church; and further that Christ is speaking in this same chapter only of the laity and not of the priests. For to the latter the living bread of heaven, that is the sacrament in one kind, does not belong, but perhaps the bread of death from hell! But what is to be done with the deacons and subdeacons,[27] who are neither laymen nor priests? According to this distinguished writer they ought to use neither the one kind nor both kinds! You see, my dear Tulich, what a novel and "Observant" method of treating Scripture this is.

But learn this too: In John 6 Christ is speaking of the Sacrament of the Altar, although he himself teaches us that he is speaking of faith in the incarnate Word, for he says: "This is the work of God, that you believe in him whom he has sent" [John 6:29]. But we'll have to give him credit: this Leipzig professor

27. Subdeacons and deacons are the fifth and sixth of the seven offices through which clergy advanced to the priesthood. Theologians debated whether these middle offices participated in the sacrament of Holy Orders until the Council of Trent decided that they did. For a discussion of the seven offices, see Martin Chemnitz, *Examination of the Council of Trent*, II:9:2 (St. Louis: Concordia, 1978).

of the Bible can prove anything he pleases from any passage of Scripture he pleases. For he is an Anaxagorian,[28] or rather an Aristotelian, theologian for whom nouns and verbs when interchanged mean the same thing and any thing.[29] Throughout the whole of his book he so fits together the testimony of the Scriptures that if he set out to prove that Christ is in the sacrament he would not hesitate to begin thus: "The lesson is from the book of the Revelation of St. John the Apostle." All his quotations are as apt as this one would be, and the wiseacre imagines he is adorning his drivel with the multitude of his quotations. The rest I will pass over, lest I smother you with the filth of this vile-smelling sewer.[k]

In conclusion, he brings forward 1 Cor. 11[:23], where Paul says that he received from the Lord and delivered to the Corinthians the use of both the bread and the cup. Here again our distinguisher of kinds, treating the Scriptures with his usual brilliance, teaches that Paul permitted, but did not deliver, the use of both kinds. Do you ask where he gets his proof? Out of his own head, as he did in the case of John 6. For it does not behoove this lecturer to give a reason for his assertions; he belongs to that order whose members prove and teach everything by their visions.[30] Accordingly we are here taught that in this passage the apostle did not write to the whole Corinthian congregation, but to the laity alone—and therefore gave no "permission" at all to the clergy, but deprived them of the sacrament altogether! Further, according to a new kind of grammar, "I have received from the Lord" means the same as "it is permitted by the Lord," and "I have delivered to you" is the same as "I have permitted to you." I pray you, mark this well. For by this method not only the church, but any worthless fellow, will be at liberty, according to this master, to turn all the universal commands, institutions, and ordinances of Christ and the apostles into mere "permission."

I perceive therefore that this man is driven by a messenger of Satan[l] and that he and his partners are seeking to make a name for themselves in the world through me, as men who are worthy to cross swords with Luther. But their hopes shall be dashed. In my contempt for them I shall never even mention their names, but content myself with this one reply to all their books. If they

28. Anaxagoras (c. 510–428 BCE) was a pre-Socratic philosopher charged with impiety for his novel interpretations of myths that he adapted to fit his naturalistic explanations of physical phenomena. Luther is using the comparison to highlight Alveld's forced interpretations of Scripture.

29. The philosophy of Aristotle (384–322 BCE) was an essential feature of Scholastic theology. Aristotle's categories, method, and scientific and ethical theories were often incorporated into the explanation of theological topics and the interpretation of Scripture. Such extensive and uncritical use of Aristotle in theology was quite controversial from the outset and a central point of Luther's early critique of Scholastic theology. Here Luther probably has in mind Aristotle's study of language, "On Interpretation," in his collection of logical treatises, the *Organon*.

30. Franciscans. St. Francis (c. 1182–1226) was known for his various visions, including the call to rebuild the ruined chapel of San Damiano that marked the beginning of his mendicant life and his vision at the end of his life on Mt. Verna which bestowed on him the *stigmata*, the five wounds of Christ.

k   *Cloaca.*

l   2 Cor. 12:7.

are worthy of it, I pray that Christ in his mercy may bring them back to a sound mind. If they are not worthy, I pray that they may never leave off writing such books, and that the enemies of truth may never deserve to read any others. There is a true and popular saying:

> "This I know for certain—whenever I fight with filth,
> victor or vanquished, I am sure to be defiled."[31]

And since I see that they have an abundance of leisure and writing paper, I shall furnish them with ample matter to write about. For I shall keep ahead of them, so that while they are triumphantly celebrating a glorious victory over one of my heresies (as it seems to them), I shall meanwhile be devising a new one. I too am desirous of seeing these illustrious leaders in battle decorated with many honors. Therefore, while they murmur that I approve of communion in both kinds, and are most happily engrossed with this important and worthy subject, I shall go one step further and undertake to show that all who deny communion in both kinds to the laity are wicked men. To do this more conveniently I shall compose *a prelude on the captivity of the Roman church*. In due time, when the most learned papists have disposed of this book I shall offer more.

I take this course, lest any pious reader who may chance upon this book, should be offended by the filthy matter with which I deal and should justly complain that he finds nothing in it which cultivates or instructs his mind or which furnishes any food for learned reflection. For you know how impatient my friends are that I waste my time on the sordid fictions of these men. They say that the mere reading of them is ample confutation; they look for better things from me, which Satan seeks to hinder through these men. I have finally resolved to follow the advice of my friends and to leave to those hornets the business of wrangling and hurling invectives.

Of that Italian friar of Cremona[m] I shall say nothing. He is an unlearned man and a simpleton, who attempts with a few rhetorical passages to recall me to the Holy See, from which I am not as yet aware of having departed, nor has anyone proved that

31. Luther used the common saying later in his edition of *Aesop's Fables* (1530). There he used it as the moral to the fable of the ass and the lion. See Carl P. E. Springer, *Luther's Aesop*, Early Modern Studies, vol. 8 (Kirksville, MO: Truman State University Press, 2011).

m Isidoro Isolani; see n. 17, p. 15 above.

I have. His chief argument in those silly passages" is that I ought to be moved by my monastic vows and by the fact that the empire has been transferred to the Germans. Thus he does not seem to have wanted to write my "recantation" so much as the praise of the French people and the Roman pontiff.[32] Let him attest his allegiance in this little book, such as it is. He does not deserve to be harshly treated, for he seems to have been prompted by no malice; nor does he deserve to be learnedly refuted, since all his chatter is sheer ignorance and inexperience.

[Central Premise]

To begin with, I must deny that there are seven sacraments, and for the present maintain that there are but three: baptism, penance, and the bread.[33] All three have been subjected to a miserable captivity by the Roman curia, and the church has been robbed of all her liberty. Yet, if I were to speak according to the usage of the Scriptures, I should have only one single sacrament,[34] but with three sacramental signs, of which I shall treat more fully at the proper time.

[The Sacrament of the Lord's Supper]

Now concerning the sacrament of the bread first of all.

I shall tell you now what progress I have made as a result of my studies on the administration of this sacrament. For at the time when I was publishing my treatise on the Eucharist,[35] I adhered to the common custom and did not concern myself at all with the question of whether the pope was right or wrong. But now that I have been challenged and attacked, no, forcibly thrust into this arena, I shall freely speak my mind, whether all the papists laugh or weep together.

In the first place the sixth chapter of John must be entirely excluded from this discussion, since it does not refer to the sacrament in a single syllable. Not only because the sacrament was not yet instituted, but even more because the passage itself and

32. On Christmas day, 800, the Frankish ruler, Charlemagne (c. 747–814), was crowned by Pope Leo III as the "Emperor of the Romans" (*Imperator Romanorum*), and since that time Germanic kings claimed continuity with the ancient Roman Empire (*translatio imperii*), even though in the East the empire continued on with its own succession of emperors in Constantinople. More specifically, Luther is here referring to the most recent election of Charles V (1500–1558) in 1519 who, though only partly German, was certainly more so than Francis I of France, the pope's preferred candidate.

33. The common designation for the Lord's Supper, especially since the cup was withheld from the laity. By the end of the treatise Luther will conclude that there are only two sacraments; see p. 127.

34. 1 Tim. 3:16: "Without any doubt, the mystery of our religion is great: He was revealed in flesh, vindicated in spirit, seen by angels, proclaimed among Gentiles, believed in throughout the world, taken up in glory." In the Latin Bible, the word *mystery* is translated with *sacramentum*. See below, n. 210, p. 98. Cf. also thesis 18 of Luther's *Disputatio fide infusa et acquisita* ("Disputation Concerning Infused and Acquired Faith"), WA 6:85–86.

35. *The Blessed Sacrament of the Holy and True Body of Christ, and the Brotherhoods* (1519), LW 35:45–74; TAL 1:225–56.

n I.e., *Revocatio Martini Lutheri Augustiniani ad sanctam sedem*; cf. n. 15.

the sentences following plainly show, as I have already stated, that Christ is speaking of faith in the incarnate Word. For he says: "My words are spirit and life" [John 6:63], which shows that he was speaking of a spiritual eating, by which he who eats has life; whereas the Jews understood him to mean a bodily eating and therefore disputed with him. But no eating can give life except that which is by faith, for that is truly a spiritual and living eating. As Augustine also says: "Why do you make ready your teeth and your stomach? Believe, and you have eaten."[36] For the sacramental eating does not give life, since many eat unworthily. Hence Christ cannot be understood in this passage to be speaking about the sacrament.

Some persons, to be sure, have misapplied these words in their teaching concerning the sacrament, as in the decretal *Dudum*[37] and many others. But it is one thing to misapply the Scriptures and another to understand them in their proper sense. Otherwise, if in this passage Christ were enjoining a sacramental eating, when he says: "Unless you eat my flesh and drink my blood, you have no life in you" [John 6:53], he would be condemning all infants, all the sick, and all those absent or in any way hindered from the sacramental eating, however strong their faith might be. Thus Augustine, in his *Contra Julianum*, Book II,[o] proves from Innocent[38] that even infants eat the flesh and drink the blood of Christ without the sacrament; that is, they partake of them through the faith of the church.[39] Let this then be accepted as proved: John 6 does not belong here. For this reason I have written elsewhere[p] that the Bohemians[40] cannot properly rely on this passage in support of the sacrament in both kinds.

Now there are two passages that do bear very clearly upon this matter: the Gospel narratives of the Lord's Supper and Paul in 1 Cor. 11[:23-25]. Let us examine these. Matt. [26:26-28], Mark [14:22-24], and Luke [22:19f.] agree that Christ gave the whole sacrament to all his disciples. That Paul delivered both kinds is so certain that no one has ever had the temerity to say otherwise. Add to this that Matt. [26:27] reports that Christ did not say of the bread, "eat of it, all of you," but of the cup, "drink of it, all of you." Mark [14:23] likewise does not say, "they all ate of it," but

36. Augustine (354–430), bishop of Hippo in North Africa, was the most influential church father in Western Christianity and remained particularly important for Luther. He is quoting from Augustine's *Sermo* 112, 5.

37. *Dudum* is the incorrect decretal. The correct reference is *Quum Marthae*, in the Decretals of Gregory IX (r. 1227–1241), lib. 3, tit. 41: *de celebratione missarum, et sacramento eucharistiae et divinis officiis,* CIC 2:636–39.

38. Pope Innocent I (d. 417).

39. Innocent's argument can be found in the letters of Augustine, *Ep.* 182, 5; CSEL 44:720.

40. Luther is referring to the followers of Jan Hus (1369–1415). After the condemnation and burning of Hus at the Council of Constance (1414–18), his successor, Jacobellus von Mies (c. 1372–1429), argued for the necessity of communion in both kinds—the bread and the cup—for salvation on the basis of John 6:54. The Bohemians were granted the use of the cup by the Council of Basel in 1433, but this was revoked by Pope Pius II (r. 1458–1464) in 1462.

o   *Against Julian* II, 36; CSEL 85¹:183f.

p   *Verklärung etlicher Artikel in einem Sermon vom heiligen Sakrament* (1520), WA 6:80.

"they all drank of it." Both attach the note of universality to the cup, not to the bread, as though the Spirit foresaw this schism, by which some would be forbidden to partake of the cup, which Christ desired should be common to all. How furiously, do you suppose, would they rave against us, if they had found the word "all" attached to the bread instead of to the cup? They would certainly leave us no loophole to escape. They would cry out and brand us as heretics and damn us as schismatics. But now, when the Scripture is on our side and against them, they will not allow themselves to be bound by any force of logic. Men of the most free will they are, even in the things that are God's; they change and change again, and throw everything into confusion.

But imagine me standing over against them and interrogating my lords, the papists. In the Lord's Supper, the whole sacrament, or communion in both kinds, is given either to the priests alone or else it is at the same time given to the laity. If it is given only to the priests (as they would have it),[41] then it is not right to give it to the laity in either kind. For it must not be given rashly to any to whom Christ did not give it when he instituted the sacrament. Otherwise, if we permit one institution of Christ to be changed, we make all of his laws invalid, and any man may make bold to say that he is not bound by any other law or institution of Christ. For a single exception, especially in the Scriptures, invalidates the whole.[q] But if it is given also to the laity, it inevitably follows that it ought not to be withheld from them in either form. And if any do withhold it from them when they ask for it they are acting impiously and contrary to the act, example, and institution of Christ.

I acknowledge that I am conquered by this argument, which to me is irrefutable. I have neither read nor heard nor found anything to say against it. For here the word and example of Christ stand unshaken when he says, not by way of permission, but of command: "Drink of it, all of you" [Matt. 26:27]. For if all are to drink of it, and the words cannot be understood as addressed to the priests alone, then it is certainly an impious act to withhold the cup from the laymen when they desire it, even though an angel from heaven were to do it.[r] For when they say that the distribution of both kinds is left to the decision of the church,

41. Gabriel Biel's (c. 1420–1495) *Exposition of the Canon of the Mass* (Lect. 84), which Luther studied extensively, makes the argument that Christ's words, "do this in remembrance of me," were directed to the disciples and their successors, the priests. Thus the cup can be withheld from the laity in order to distinguish them from the clergy.

q   Perhaps a reference to James 2:10.
r   Cf. Gal. 1:8.

42. Luther is speaking in the person of his opponents.

43. Thomas Aquinas (1225–1274), a Dominican theologian at the University of Paris, maintained that though there are several signs in the sacrament, namely, the bread and wine, this does not constitute two but only one complete sacrament. Both are necessary for the spiritual refreshment offered; *STh* III, q. 73, a. 2: "The bread and wine are materially several signs, yet formally and perfectively one, inasmuch as one refreshment is prepared therefrom." Regarding the communion of priests, in canon 5 of the Twelfth Council of Toledo (681 CE) it is required that the celebrating priest must receive both the body and blood of Christ. Likewise, there is a prohibition against dividing the sacrament in the twelfth-century *Decretum Gratiani*, pt. III, *de Consecratione*, d. 2, chap. 12: "Let them either receive the sacraments entire or be excluded from the entire sacraments, for a division of one and the same sacrament cannot be made without great sacrilege." Aquinas, aware of both, makes the same point in *STh* III, q. 82, a. 4.

44. The words of Christ in the *Canon of the Mass* harmonized the reading of Matt. 26:28, "poured out for many" (which is very possibly a reference to Isa. 53:12, "yet he bore the sin of many"), and Luke 22:20, "poured for you."

they make this assertion without reason and put it forth without authority. It can be ignored just as readily as it can be proved. It is of no avail against an opponent who confronts us with the word and work of Christ; he must be refuted with the word of Christ, but this we[42] do not possess.

If, however, either kind may be withheld from the laity, then with equal right and reason a part of baptism or penance might also be taken away from them by this same authority of the church. Therefore, just as baptism and absolution must be administered in their entirety, so the sacrament of the bread must be given in its entirety to all laymen, if they desire it. I am much amazed, however, by their assertion that the priests may never receive only one kind in the Mass under pain of mortal sin; and that for no other reason except (as they unanimously say) that the two kinds constitute one complete sacrament, which may not be divided.[43] I ask them, therefore, to tell me why it is lawful to divide it in the case of the laity, and why they are the only ones to whom the entire sacrament is not given? Do they not acknowledge, by their own testimony, either that both kinds are to be given to the laity or that the sacrament is not valid when only one kind is given to them? How can it be that the sacrament in one kind is not complete in the case of the priests, yet in the case of the laity it is complete? Why do they flaunt the authority of the church and the power of the pope in my face? These do not annul the words of God and the testimony of the truth.

It follows, further, that if the church can withhold from the laity one kind, the wine, it can also withhold from them the other, the bread. It could therefore withhold the entire Sacrament of the Altar from the laity and completely annul Christ's institution as far as they are concerned. By what authority, I ask. If the church cannot withhold the bread, or both kinds, neither can it withhold the wine. This cannot possibly be disputed; for the church's power must be the same over either kind as it is over both kinds, and if it has no power over both kinds, it has none over either kind. I am curious to hear what the flatterers of Rome will have to say to this.

But what carries most weight with me, however, and is quite decisive for me is that Christ says: "This is my blood, which is poured out for you and for many for the forgiveness of sins."[44] Here you see very clearly that the blood is given to all those for whose sins it was poured out. But who will dare to say that it was not poured out for the laity? And do you not see whom he addresses when he gives the cup? Does he not give it to all? Does he not say that it is poured out for all? "For you" [Luke 22:20], he says—let this refer to the priests. "And for many" [Matt. 26:28], however, cannot possibly refer to the priests. Yet he says: "Drink of it, all of you" [Matt. 26:27]. I too could easily trifle here and with my words make a mockery of Christ's words, as my dear trifler[s] does. But those who rely on the Scriptures in opposing us must be refuted by the Scriptures.

This is what has prevented me from condemning the Bohemians,[t] who, whether they are wicked men or good, certainly have the word and act of Christ on their side, while we have neither, but only that inane remark of men: "The church has so ordained." It was not the church which ordained these things, but the tyrants of the churches, without the consent of the church, which is the people of God.

But now I ask, where is the necessity, where is the religious duty, where is the practical use of denying both kinds, that is, the visible sign, to the laity, when everyone concedes to them the grace of the sacrament without the sign?[u] If they concede the grace, which is the greater, why not the sign, which is the lesser? For in every sacrament the sign as such is incomparably less than the thing signified. What then, I ask, is to prevent them from conceding the lesser, when they concede the greater? Unless indeed, as it seems to me, it has come about by the permission of an angry God in order to give occasion for a schism in the church, to bring home to us how, having long ago lost the grace of the sacrament, we contend for the sign, which is the lesser, against that which is the most important and the chief thing; just as some men for the sake of ceremonies contend against love.[v] This monstrous perversion seems to date from the time

---

s   Alveld, cf. n. 14, p. 15.

t   See n. 40, p. 22.

u   E.g., Augustine, *Sermo* 272; Peter Lombard, *Sentences* 4, d. 1, c. 2-4; Aquinas, *STh* III, q. 80, a. 1; Gabriel Biel, *Sentences* 4, d. 1, q.1, a.1, n. 1; Cf. *STh* III, q. 79, a. 4: "Two things may be considered in this sacrament, namely, the sacrament itself (*ipsum sacramentum*), and the reality of the sacrament (*res sacramenti*) . . . the reality of this sacrament is charity (*res autem huius sacramenti est caritas*)."

v   Perhaps a reference to Matt. 15:1-9.

when we began to rage against Christian love for the sake of the riches of this world. Thus God would show us, by this terrible sign, how we esteem signs more than the things they signify. How preposterous it would be to admit that the faith of baptism is granted to the candidate for baptism, and yet to deny him the sign of this very faith, namely, the water!

Finally, Paul stands invincible and stops the mouth of everyone when he says in 1 Cor. 11[:23]: "For I received from the Lord what I also delivered to you." He does not say: "I permitted to you," as this friar[45] of ours lyingly asserts out of his own head. Nor is it true that Paul delivered both kinds on account of the contention among the Corinthians. In the first place, the text shows that their contention was not about the reception of both kinds, but about the contempt and envy between rich and poor. The text clearly states: "One is hungry and another is drunk, and you humiliate those who have nothing" [1 Cor. 11:21-22]. Moreover, Paul is not speaking of the time when he first delivered the sacrament to them, for he does not say "I receive from the Lord" and "I give to you," but "I received" and "I delivered"—namely, when he first began to preach among them, a long while before this contention. This shows that he delivered both kinds to them, for "delivered" means the same as "commanded," for elsewhere he uses the word in this sense.[46] Consequently there is nothing in the friar's fuming about permission; he has raked it together without Scripture, without reason, without sense. His opponents do not ask what he has dreamed, but what the Scriptures decree in the matter, and out of the Scriptures he cannot adduce one jot or tittle in support of his dreams, while they can produce mighty thunderbolts in support of their faith.

Rise up then, you popish flatterers, one and all! Get busy and defend yourselves against the charges of impiety, tyranny, and treason[w] against the gospel, and of the crime of slandering your brethren. You decry as heretics those who refuse to contravene such plain and powerful words of Scripture in order to acknowledge the mere dreams of your brains! If any are to be called heretics and schismatics, it is not the Bohemians or the Greeks,[47] for they take their stand upon the Gospels. It is you Romans who are the heretics and godless schismatics, for you presume upon

45. Luther is still dealing with Alveld's argument.

46. 1 Cor. 11:1 in the Vulgate reads, "but I praise you brothers that you remember me in everything and keep my *commandments* just as I *delivered* them to you" (*laudo autem vos fratres quod omnia mei memores estis et sicut tradidi vobis praecepta mea tenetis*).

47. That is, the Eastern Orthodox Church, which split from the Western church in 1054. In the Eastern Rite, both kinds in the sacrament are administered to the faithful with the eucharistic spoon.

w   Or "lèse-majesté," from the Latin, *laesa maiestate*; literally, "having caused injury to the sovereignty," in this case of the gospel.

your figments alone against the clear Scriptures of God. Wash yourself of that, men!

But what could be more ridiculous and more worthy of this friar's brains than his saying that the Apostle wrote these words and gave this permission, not to the church universal, but to a particular church, that is, the Corinthian? Where does he get his proof? Out of one storehouse, his own impious head. If the church universal receives, reads, and follows this epistle as written for itself in all other respects, why should it not do the same with this portion also? If we admit that any epistle, or any part of any epistle, of Paul does not apply to the church universal, then the whole authority of Paul falls to the ground. Then the Corinthians will say that what he teaches about faith in the Epistle to the Romans does not apply to them. What greater blasphemy and madness can be imagined than this! God forbid that there should be one jot or tittle in all of Paul which the whole church universal is not bound to follow and keep! The fathers never held an opinion like this, not even down to these perilous times of which Paul was speaking when he foretold that there would be blasphemers and blind, insensate men.[x] This friar is one of them, perhaps even the chief.

However, suppose we grant the truth of this intolerable madness. If Paul gave his permission to a particular church, then, even from your own point of view, the Greeks and Bohemians are in the right, for they are particular churches. Hence it is sufficient that they do not act contrary to Paul, who at least gave permission. Moreover, Paul could not permit anything contrary to Christ's institution. Therefore, O Rome, I cast in your teeth, and in the teeth of all your flatterers, these sayings of Christ and Paul, on behalf of the Greeks and the Bohemians. I defy you to prove that you have been given any authority to change these things by as much as one hair, much less to accuse others of heresy because they disregard your arrogance. It is rather you who deserve to be charged with the crime of godlessness and despotism.

Concerning this point we may read Cyprian,[48] who alone is strong enough to refute all the Romanists. In the fifth book of his treatise *On the Lapsed,* he testifies that it was the widespread

48. Cyprian (c. 200–258) was bishop of Carthage during the Decian persecution (250–251). In dealing with the lapsed Christians who desired readmittance, Cyprian tried to steer a middle course between laxist and rigorist positions. The treatise *De lapsis* ("On the Lapsed") was written c. 251–252. Cyprian was martyred during the Valerian persecution on 14 September 258.

x 2 Tim. 3:1-9.

custom in that church [at Carthage] to administer both kinds to the laity, even to children, indeed, to give the body of the Lord into their hands. And of this he gives many examples. Among other things, he reproves some of the people as follows: "The sacrilegious man is angered at the priests because he does not immediately receive the body of the Lord with unclean hands, or drink the blood of the Lord with unclean lips." He is speaking here, you see, of irreverent laymen who desired to receive the body and the blood from the priests. Do you find anything to snarl at here, wretched flatterer? Will you say that this holy martyr, a doctor of the church endowed with the apostolic spirit, was a heretic, and that he used this permission in a particular church?

In the same place Cyprian narrates an incident that came under his own observation. He describes at length how a deacon was administering the cup to a little girl,[49] and when she drew away from him he poured the blood of the Lord into her mouth.[y] We read the same of St. Donatus, and how trivially does this wretched flatterer dispose of his broken chalice![50] "I read of a broken chalice," he says, "but I do not read that the blood was administered."[51] No wonder! He that finds what he pleases in the Holy Scriptures will also read what he pleases in the histories. But can the authority of the church be established, or the heretics be refuted, in this way?

But enough on this subject! I did not undertake this work for the purpose of answering one who is not worthy of a reply, but to bring the truth of the matter to light.

I conclude, then, that it is wicked and despotic to deny both kinds to the laity, and that this is not within the power of any angel, much less of any pope or council. Nor does the Council of Constance give me pause, for if its authority is valid, why not that of the Council of Basel as well, which decreed to the contrary that the Bohemians should be permitted to receive the sacrament in both kinds?[52] That decision was reached only after considerable discussion, as the extant records and documents of the Council show. And to this Council the ignorant flatterer refers in support of his dream; with such wisdom does he handle the whole matter.

---

49. The Latin, *infanti*, indicates a child under the age of seven.

50. Donatus (d. c. 372), not to be confused with the schismatic bishop of Carthage, was bishop of Arezzo. According to one legend, Donatus was celebrating the Eucharist with a glass chalice when, during a sudden attack by pagan intruders, the chalice was shattered. Miraculously, Donatus was able to reassemble the chalice immediately and even with a missing piece continue the celebration.

51. Alveld uses the story in his *Tractatus* to argue against the cup being administered to the laity.

52. The Council of Constance (1414–1418) adjudicated the case of Jan Hus and the Bohemian practice of communion in both kinds. The Council upheld the practice of withholding the cup and condemned Hus, burning him at the stake as a heretic. Alveld cited the decrees of the council in his *Tractatus*. On the other hand, the Council of Basel granted the Bohemians special privilege for the administration of the sacrament in both kinds in 1433.

y   *De lapsis* 25; CSEL 31, 255. Augustine also mentions the story in a letter: *Ep.* 98,4; CSEL 34 II, 524–26.

[The First Captivity: Withholding the Cup]

The first captivity of this sacrament, therefore, concerns its substance or completeness, which the tyranny of Rome has wrested from us. Not that those who use only one kind sin against Christ, for Christ did not command the use of either kind, but left it to the choice of each individual, when he said: "As often as you do this, do it in remembrance of me" [1 Cor. 11:25]. But they are the sinners, who forbid the giving of both kinds to those who wish to exercise this choice. The fault lies not with the laity, but with the priests. The sacrament does not belong to the priests, but to everyone. The priests are not lords but servants whose duty is to administer both kinds to those who desire them, as often as they desire them. If they wrest this right from the laity and deny it to them by force, they are tyrants; but the laity are without fault, whether they lack one kind or both kinds. In the meantime they must be preserved by their faith and by their desire for the complete sacrament.[53] These same servants are likewise bound to administer baptism and absolution to everyone who seeks them, because he has a right to them; but if they do not administer them, the seeker has the full merit of his faith, while they will be accused before Christ as wicked servants. Thus the holy fathers of old in the desert did not receive the sacrament in any form for many years at a time.[z]

Therefore I do not urge that both kinds be seized upon by force, as if we were bound to this form by a rigorous command, but I instruct men's consciences so that they may endure

In this polyptych (1320) by Pietro Lorenzetti (1280–1348), St. Donatus is pictured (far left) at the Church of Santa Maria della Pieve in Arezzo, Tuscany.

53. Cf. Aquinas, *STh* III, q. 80, a.1: "the effect of the sacrament can be secured by every man if he receive it in desire, though not in reality. Consequently, just as some are baptized with the baptism of desire, through their desire of baptism, before being baptized in the baptism of water; so likewise some eat this sacrament spiritually ere they receive it sacramentally. Now this happens in two ways. First of all, from desire of receiving the sacrament itself, and thus are said to be baptized, and to eat spiritually, and not sacramentally,

z   Cf. Luther's *A Treatise Concerning the Ban*, LW 39:3–22.

they who desire to receive these sacraments since they have been instituted. Secondly, by a figure: thus the Apostle says (1 Corinthians 10:2), that the fathers of old were 'baptized in the cloud and in the sea,' and that 'they did eat . . . spiritual food, and . . . drank . . . spiritual drink.' Nevertheless, sacramental eating is not without avail, because the actual receiving of the sacrament produces more fully the effect of the sacrament than does the desire thereof, as stated above of baptism."

54. John Wycliffe (c. 1331–1384), an English Scholastic theologian and philosopher at Oxford, was an early critic of the doctrine of transubstantiation. For this and a variety of other positions, Wycliffe was posthumously declared a heretic at the Council of Constance on 4 May 1415. Later, in 1428, his body was exhumed and burned.

55. Pierre d'Ailly (1350–1420), chancellor of the University of Paris and cardinal of Cambrai, was an influential Scholastic theologian in the Occamist tradition. Luther studied his *Questiones quarti libri sententiarum* in his early career as a student of theology in Erfurt.

56. The *Sentences* of Peter Lombard (c. 1096–1160) was the standard text for medieval Scholastic theology. Prominent theologians would often publish their own commentaries on Lombard's *Sentences*, which then became the focus of subsequent study and comment.

57. "Accident" refers to the property or quality of a thing that does not touch upon its essential nature or substance. This is an Aristotelian distinction that attained common usage in medieval

the Roman tyranny, knowing well that they have been forcibly deprived of their rightful share in the sacrament because of their own sin. This only do I desire—that no one should justify the tyranny of Rome, as if it were doing right in forbidding one kind to the laity. We ought rather to abhor it, withhold our consent, and endure it just as we should do if we were held captive by the Turk and not permitted to use either kind. This is what I meant by saying that it would be a good thing, in my opinion, if this captivity were ended by the decree of a general council,[a] our Christian liberty restored to us out of the hands of the Roman tyrant, and everyone left free to seek and receive this sacrament, just as we are free to receive baptism and penance. But now we are compelled by the same tyranny to receive the one kind year after year, so utterly lost is the liberty which Christ has given us. This is the due reward of our godless ingratitude.

[The Second Captivity: Transubstantiation]

The second captivity of this sacrament is less grievous as far as the conscience is concerned, yet the gravest of dangers threatens the person who would attack it, to say nothing of condemning it. Here I shall be called a Wycliffite[54] and a heretic by six hundred names. But what of it? Since the Roman bishop has ceased to be a bishop and has become a tyrant, I fear none of his decrees; for I know that it is not within his power, nor that of any general council, to make new articles of faith.[b]

Some time ago, when I was drinking in scholastic theology, the learned Cardinal of Cambrai[55] gave me food for thought in his comments on the fourth book of the *Sentences*.[56] He argues with great acumen that to hold that real bread and real wine, and not merely their accidents,[57] are present on the altar, would be much more probable and require fewer superfluous miracles—if only the church had not decreed otherwise. When I learned later

---

a   See n. 52, p. 28.

b   See Luther's *On the Councils and the Church* in this volume, pp. 317–443.

c   The Latin saying is *inter sacrum et saxum*—literally, "between the sacred thing (i.e., sacrificial victim) and the stone knife." The meaning here is that when in such a position, hesitation due to uncertainty is extremely dangerous. Cf. Erasmus, *Adagia* 1, 1, 15.

what church it was that had decreed this, namely, the Thomistic[58]—that is, the Aristotelian church—I grew bolder, and having lingered "between knife and sacrifice,"[c] I at last found rest for my conscience in the above view, namely, that it is real bread and real wine, in which Christ's real flesh and real blood are present in no other way and to no less a degree than the others assert them to be under their accidents. I reached this conclusion because I saw that the opinions of the Thomists, whether approved by pope or by council,[59] remain only opinions, and would not become articles of faith even if an angel from heaven were to decree otherwise.[60] For what is asserted without the Scriptures or proven revelation may be held as an opinion, but need not be believed. But this opinion of Thomas hangs so completely in the air without support of Scripture or reason that it seems to me he knows neither his philosophy nor his logic. For Aristotle speaks of subject and accidents so very differently from St. Thomas that it seems to me this great man is to be pitied not only for attempting to draw his opinions in matters of faith from Aristotle, but also for attempting to base them upon a man whom he did not understand, thus building an unfortunate superstructure upon an unfortunate foundation.[61]

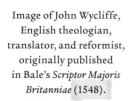

Image of John Wycliffe, English theologian, translator, and reformist, originally published in Bale's *Scriptor Majoris Britanniae* (1548).

theology; see for example Lombard, *Sentences* 4, d. 12, c. 1. In the doctrine of transubstantiation, the "accidents" of the bread and wine—i.e., their appearance, smell, and taste—are said to remain while the "substance" is miraculously changed into Christ's body and blood through consecration. Luther is probably referring to d'Ailly's comments in *Sentences* 4, qu. 6 J; however, see Leif Grane, "Luthers Kritik an Thomas von Aquin in 'De captivate Babylonica,'" *Zeitschrift für Kirchengeschichte* (1969): 3 n.7.

58. Thomas Aquinas (see n. 43 above) was known for his reliance on Aristotle in his attempt to demonstrate a synthesis between philosophy and theology. His articulation of the doctrine of transubstantiation came to be the most influential in the medieval church. See *STh* III, q. 75.

59. In 1215, the Fourth Lateran Council referred to the bread and wine as "transubstantiated" into the body and blood of Christ. Pope Innocent III presided over this council. An official decree on the doctrine of transubstantiation was not arrived at until the Council of Trent in 1551.

60. See Gal. 1:8: "But even if we or an angel from heaven should preach to you a gospel contrary to the one we preached to you, let him be accursed."

61. Aristotle did not conceive of accidental qualities existing apart from the substance; they are de facto a quality of a prior substance. Aquinas is aware of this difficulty; citing Aristotle, however, he appeals to divine providence and the power of God to dispense with this logical problem. Nonetheless, this is precisely the problem for Luther: Why insist on using

Aristotle as an aid to theology if one must dispense with it precisely in the moment of theological difficulty?

62. Some of Luther's most important writings on these topics since 1517: *Disputation Against Scholastic Theology* (1517); *[Ninety-Five Theses or] Disputation for Clarifying the Power of Indulgences* (1517); *A Sermon on Indulgences and Grace* (1518); *The Heidelberg Disputation* (1518); *Treatise on Good Works* (1520). See TAL, vol. 1.

63. See 2 Tim. 3:8: "As Jannes and Jambres opposed Moses, so these people, of corrupt mind and counterfeit faith [*reprobi circa fidem*], also oppose the truth."

64. Origen (c. 184–253) was a theologian who taught in the catechetical school in Alexandria. He was a prolific interpreter of the Scriptures and perhaps the most influential biblical commentator in the Western church. He helped shape principles for recognizing multiple spiritual meanings in the biblical text, commonly referred to as the allegorical approach to the Bible. While this approach was not without controversy, questions of orthodoxy focused primarily on Origen's theological speculation regarding the origin of the soul and the equality of the Son with the Father. He was posthumously condemned of heresy in the sixth century.

Therefore I permit everyone to hold either of these opinions, as he or she chooses. My one concern at present is to remove all scruples of conscience, so that they need not fear being called heretics if they believe that real bread and real wine are present on the altar,[d] and that everyone may feel at liberty to ponder, hold, and believe either one view or the other without endangering one's salvation. However, I shall now set forth my own view.

In the first place, I do not intend to listen or attach the least importance to those who will cry out that this teaching of mine is Wycliffite, Hussite, heretical, and contrary to the decree of the church. No one will do this except those very persons whom I have convicted of manifold heresies in the matter of indulgences, freedom of the will and the grace of God, good works and sins, etc.[62] If Wycliffe was once a heretic, they are heretics ten times over; and it is a pleasure to be blamed and accused by heretics and perverse sophists, since to please them would be the height of impiety. Besides, the only way in which they can prove their opinions and disprove contrary ones is by saying: "That is Wycliffite, Hussite, heretical!" They carry this feeble argument always on the tip of their tongues, and they have nothing else. If you ask for scriptural proof, they say: "This is our opinion, and the church (that is, we ourselves) has decided thus." To such an extent these men, who are reprobate concerning the faith[63] and untrustworthy, have the effrontery to set their own fancies before us in the name of the church as articles of faith.

But there are good grounds for my view, and this above all—no violence is to be done to the words of God, whether by human or angel.[e] They are to be retained in their simplest meaning as far as possible. Unless the context manifestly compels it, they are not to be understood apart from their grammatical and proper

---

d   The original of this part of the sentence is singular.

e   Gal. 1:8.

sense, lest we give our adversaries occasion to make a mockery of all the Scriptures. Thus Origen was rightly repudiated long ago because, ignoring the grammatical sense, he turned the trees and everything else written concerning Paradise into allegories, from which one could have inferred that trees were not created by God.[64] Even so here, when the Evangelists plainly write that Christ took bread [Matt. 26:26; Mark 14:22; Luke 22:19] and blessed it, and when the Book of Acts and the Apostle Paul in turn call it bread [Acts 2:46; 20:7; 1 Cor. 10:16; 11:23, 26-28], we have to think of real bread and real wine, just as we do of a real cup (for even they do not say that the cup was transubstantiated). Since it is not necessary, therefore, to assume a transubstantiation effected by divine power, it must be regarded as a figment of the human mind, for it rests neither on the Scriptures nor on reason, as we shall see.

Therefore it is an absurd and unheard-of juggling with words to understand "bread" to mean "the form or accidents of bread," and "wine" to mean "the form or accidents of wine."[65] Why do they not also understand all other things to mean their "forms or accidents"? And even if this might be done with all other things, it would still not be right to enfeeble the words of God in this way, and by depriving them of their meaning to cause so much harm.

Moreover, the church kept the true faith for more than twelve hundred years, during which time the holy fathers never, at any time or place, mentioned this transubstantiation (an unnatural[f] word and a dream), until the pseudo philosophy of Aristotle began to make its inroads into the church in these last three hundred years.[66] During this time many things have been wrongly defined, as, for example, that the divine essence is neither begotten nor begets;[67] that the soul is the substantial form of the

65. E.g., Aquinas, *STh* III, q. 75, a. 5: "It is evident to sense that all the accidents of the bread and wine remain after the consecration. And this is reasonably done by divine providence. . . . Christ's flesh and blood are set before us to be partaken of under the species of those things which are the more commonly used by men, namely, bread and wine." See also n. 74, p. 35 ["accident"].

66. The prominence of Aristotle in medieval theology came from several tributaries. The use of dialectic for resolving contradictory statements from various theological authorities became increasingly necessary during the Carolingian period. What was already known of Aristotle was prized for this endeavor as can be seen in such early theological logicians as Peter Abelard (1079–1142). In a relatively short period of time, however, a vast corpus of Aristotle's writings were discovered, coming into the Latin church via the Crusades, the reconquest of Muslim Spain, and various scholarly interactions in the Mediterranean provinces of Venice and Sicily. The result was a widespread effort to bring Aristotle's method and conclusions into conformation with theological doctrine in order to help clarify and defend Christian truth.

67. Lombard, *Sentences* 1, d. 5, c. 1: "In consensus with Catholic expounders, we say regarding this that neither did the Father generate a divine essence, nor did a divine essence generate the Son, nor did a divine essence generate an essence. And here by the term 'essence' we understand the divine nature, which is common to the three persons and is whole in each of them."

f   *Portentoso.* This word could also be translated "monstrous."

Aristotle portrayed in the 1493 *Nuremberg Chronicle* as a scholar of the fifteenth century.

68. Aquinas, *STh* I, q. 76, a. 1: "Therefore this principle by which we primarily understand, whether it be called the intellect or the intellectual soul, is the form of the body. This is the demonstration used by Aristotle (*De anima* ii, 2)."

69. Pierre d'Ailly, *Sentences* 1, q. 5 E: "[The church] is not able to clearly conclude [these ideas on divine generation] from the canonical Scriptures. But if God wanted such truths [about divine generation] to be believed by catholics, then he himself would reveal [them] to the church and through [such a revelation] define [them]. Thus sometimes definitions of the church do not always proceed through obvious conclusions drawn from the Scriptures, but by a special revelation given to catholics."

70. Aquinas, *STh* III, q. 75, a. 2: "Some have held that the substance of the bread and wine remains in this sacrament after the consecration. But this opinion cannot stand . . . because it would be opposed to the veneration of this sacrament, if any substance were there, which could not be adored with adoration of *latria*."

human body.[68] These and like assertions are made without any reason or cause, as the Cardinal of Cambrai himself admits.[69]

Perhaps they will say that the danger of idolatry demands that the bread and wine should not be really present.[70] How ridiculous! The laymen have never become familiar with their subtle philosophy of substance and accidents, and could not grasp it if it were taught to them. Besides, there is the same danger in the accidents which remain and which they see, as in the case of the substance which they do not see. If they do not worship the accidents, but the Christ hidden under them, why should they worship the substance of the bread, which they do not see?

And why could not Christ include his body in the substance of the bread just as well as in the accidents? In red-hot iron, for instance, the two substances, fire and iron, are so mingled that every part is both iron and fire.[71] Why is it not even more possible that the body of Christ be contained in every part of the substance of the bread?

What will they reply? Christ is believed to have been born from the inviolate womb of his mother.[72] Let them say here too that the flesh of the Virgin was meanwhile annihilated, or as they would more aptly say, transubstantiated, so that Christ, after being enfolded in its accidents, finally came forth through the accidents! The same thing will have to be said of the shut door[g] and of the closed mouth of the sepulcher,[h] through which he went in and out without disturbing them.

Out of this has arisen that Babel of a philosophy of a constant quantity distinct from the substance,[73] until it has come to such a pass that they themselves no longer know what are accidents and what is substance. For who has ever proved beyond the shadow of a doubt that heat, color, cold, light, weight, or shape are mere accidents? Finally, they have been driven to pretend that a new substance is created by God for those accidents on the altar, all on account of Aristotle, who says: "It is the nature of an accident to be in something,"[74] and endless other monstrosities. They would be rid of all these if they simply permitted real bread to be present. I rejoice greatly that the simple faith of this sacrament is still to be found, at least among the common people. For as they do not understand, neither do they dispute whether accidents are present without substance, but believe with a simple faith that Christ's body and blood are truly contained there, and leave to those who have nothing else to do the argument about what contains them.

But perhaps they will say: "Aristotle teaches that in an affirmative proposition subject and predicate must be identical," or (to quote the wild beast's own words in the sixth book of his *Metaphysics*): "An affirmative proposition requires the agreement

71. The analogy of fire and iron was not uncommon to describe a variety of consubstantial relationships in theology; for example, Origen when describing the possibility of the incarnation in *Concerning First Principles* 2, 6, 6: "the metal iron is capable of cold and heat. If, then, a mass of iron be kept constantly in the fire, receiving the heat through all its pores and veins, and the fire being continuous and the iron never removed from it."

72. The view that not only Christ's conception but also his birth occurred with his mother's virginity intact can already be found in the second-century *Protoevangelium of James*. Many others also speak of Mary as "ever-Virgin," including Origen, Hilary of Poitiers (c. 300–c. 368), Athanasius (c. 296–373), Epiphanius of Salamis (c. 310–403), Jerome (c. 347–420), Didymus the Blind (c. 313–398), and Augustine. Likewise, Luther would continue to use the title "the ever-Virgin Mary."

73. Because in the doctrine of transubstantiation the accidents of the bread and wine remain without the substance, one must now posit the accidental property of quantity purely in relation to other accidental properties. Accidental properties (e.g., quantity) without essential properties (e.g., substance) would be an absurdity according to the *Categories* of Aristotle.

74. Aristotle, *Metaphysics* 4, 30, 1: "'Accident' means that which attaches to something and can be truly predicated, but neither of necessity nor usually." See also Aquinas, *STh* I, q. 28, a. 2: "For the essence of an accident is to inhere [in something]."

g   John 10:19, 26.
h   Matt. 28:2-6.

75. It is not Aristotle's *Metaphysics* but his *Organon*; namely, the sixth book of *Concerning Interpretation* which contains this proposition.

76. Aristotle identifies nine categories of accidents: quantity, quality, relation, place, time, position, state, action, and affection.

77. Aristotle, *Metaphysics* 7, 3: "The word 'substance' is applied, if not in more senses, still at least in four ways; for the essence and the universal and the genus are thought to be the substance of each thing, and fourthly the subject. Now the subject is that of which everything else is predicated, while it is itself not predicated of anything else."

78. Luther is pointing out how relying simply on logical categories and the rules of philosophical language will not bring one nearer to Christian truth. By positing "transaccidentation," Luther shows how the requirements of logic can remain intact even while setting forth absurd theological statements.

79. That is, the accidental properties of the eucharistic host: white and round.

80. Luther is here appealing to the grammatical agreement between the demonstrative pronoun, *hic* ("this"), and *calix* ("cup"), which are both masculine. With the correlation of cup and blood with the demonstrative pronoun, Luther seems to be saying that the continued presence of the wine is indicated in the very words of Christ.

of the subject and the predicate."[75] They interpret agreement to mean identity. Hence, when I say: "This is my body," the subject cannot be identical with the bread, but must be identical with the body of Christ.

What shall we say when Aristotle and these human doctrines are made to be the arbiters of such lofty and divine matters? Why do we not put aside such curiosity and cling simply to the words of Christ, willing to remain in ignorance of what takes place here and content that the real body of Christ is present by virtue of the words? Or is it necessary to comprehend the manner of the divine working in every detail?

But what do they say when Aristotle admits that all of the categories of accidents[76] are themselves a subject—although he grants that substance is the chief subject? Hence for him "this white," "this large," "this something" are all subjects, of which something is predicated.[77] If that is correct, I ask: If a "transubstantiation" must be assumed in order that Christ's body may not be identified with the bread, why not also a "transaccidentation," in order that the body of Christ may not be identified with the accidents?[78] For the same danger remains if one understands the subject to be "this white or this round is my body."[79] And for the same reason that a "transubstantiation" must be assumed, a "transaccidentation" must also be assumed, because of this identity of subject and predicate.

If, however, merely by an act of the intellect, you can do away with the accident, so that it will not be regarded as the subject when you say, "this is my body," why not with equal ease transcend the substance of the bread, if you do not want it to be regarded either as the subject, so that "this my body" is no less in the substance than in the accident? After all, this is a divine work performed by God's almighty power, which can operate just as much and just as well in the accident as it can in the substance.

Let us not dabble too much in philosophy, however. Does not Christ appear to have anticipated this curiosity admirably by saying of the wine, not *Hoc est sanguis meus*, but *Hic est sanguis meus*? [Mark 14:24]. He speaks even more clearly when he brings in the word "cup" and says: "This cup [*Hic calix*] is the new testament in my blood" [Luke 22:20; 1 Cor. 11:25].[80] Does it not seem as though he desired to keep us in a simple faith, sufficient for us to believe that his blood was in the cup? For my part, if I cannot fathom how the bread is the body of Christ, yet I will take my reason captive to the obedience of Christ,[i] and clinging simply to his words, firmly believe not only that the body of Christ is in the bread, but that the bread is the body of Christ. My warrant for this is the words which say: "He took bread, and when he had given thanks, he broke it and said, 'Take, eat, this (that is, this bread, which he had taken and broken) is my body'" [1 Cor. 11:23-24]. And Paul says: "The bread which we break, is it not a participation in the body of Christ?" [1 Cor. 10:16]. He does not say "in the bread there is," but "the bread itself is the participation in the body of Christ." What does it matter if philosophy cannot fathom this? The Holy Spirit is greater than Aristotle. Does philosophy fathom their transubstantiation? Why, they themselves admit that here all philosophy breaks down.[81] That the pronoun "this," in both Greek and Latin, is referred to "body" is due to the fact that in both of these languages the two words are of the same gender. In Hebrew, however, which has no neuter gender, "this" is referred to "bread," so that it would be proper to say *Hic* [bread] *est corpus meum*. Actually, the idiom of the language and common sense both prove that the subject ["this"] obviously points to the bread and not to the body, when he says: *Hoc est corpus meum—das ist meyn leyp*—that is, "This very bread here [*iste panis*] is my body."

Thus, what is true in regard to Christ is also true in regard to the sacrament. In order for the divine nature to dwell in him bodily [Col. 2:9], it is not necessary for the human nature to be transubstantiated and the divine nature contained under the accidents of the human nature. Both natures are simply there in their entirety, and it is truly said: "This man is God; this God is man." Even though philosophy cannot grasp this, faith grasps it nonetheless. And the authority of God's Word is greater than the capacity of our intellect to grasp it. In like manner, it is not necessary in the sacrament that the bread and wine be transubstantiated and that Christ be contained under their accidents in order that the real body and real blood may be present. But both remain there at the same time, and it is truly said: "This bread is my body; this wine is my blood," and vice versa. Thus I will understand it for the time being to the honor of the holy words of God, to which I will allow no violence to be done by

81. E.g., Gabriel Biel, *Sentences* 4, d. 11, q. 1, a. 3, dub. 6 N: "Because this cessation [of the substance of the bread] is supernatural and miraculous, one does not have a concept to impose from philosophy, but is able to speak about the cessation of the thing according to the whole."

i   2 Cor. 10:5.

82. Luther is referring to the first canon of the Fourth Lateran Council (1215), which uses the term *transubstantiation*: "His body and blood are truly contained in the sacrament of the altar under the forms of bread and wine, the bread and wine having been changed in substance (*transubstantiatis*), by God's power, into his body and blood, so that in order to achieve this mystery of unity we receive from God what he received from us." *Firmiter, Decretalium Gregorii IX, lib. I, tit I: de summa trinitate et fide catholica,* cap. 1, sec 3.

83. A "participation" was the notion that one could, without being present, obtain spiritual benefits from the saying of Masses. For example, such was possible with the regular Masses said in monasteries.

84. Confraternities that paid to have Masses said for them alongside other devotional practices for the purpose of gaining merit. The benefits accrued by one member through his devotion and attendance at Masses was then made available to all other members. See Luther's critique of this practice in his treatise *The Blessed Sacrament of the Holy and True Body of Christ, and the Brotherhoods* (1519), LW 35:45–74; TAL 1:225–56.

85. "Anniversaries" can refer to a year of daily Masses said on behalf of the soul of a deceased person or to Masses said every year on the anniversary of one's death.

86. Masses for the dead said on memorial days.

petty human arguments, nor will I allow them to be twisted into meanings which are foreign to them. At the same time, I permit other men to follow the other opinion, which is laid down in the decree *Firmiter*,[82] only let them not press us to accept their opinions as articles of faith (as I have said above).

[The Third Captivity: The Mass as a Sacrifice]

The third captivity of this sacrament is by far the most wicked abuse of all, in consequence of which there is no opinion more generally held or more firmly believed in the church today than this, that the Mass is a good work and a sacrifice. And this abuse has brought an endless host of other abuses in its train, so that the faith of this sacrament has become utterly extinct and the holy sacrament has been turned into mere merchandise, a market, and a profit-making business. Hence participations,[83] brotherhoods,[84] intercessions, merits, anniversaries,[85] memorial days,[86] and similar goods are bought and sold, traded and bartered, in the church. On these the priests and monks depend for their entire livelihood.

I am attacking a difficult matter, an abuse perhaps impossible to uproot, since through century-long custom and the common consent of men it has become so firmly entrenched that it would be necessary to abolish most of the books now in vogue, and to alter almost the entire external form of the churches[87] and introduce, or rather reintroduce, totally different kinds of ceremonies. But my Christ lives, and we must be careful to give more heed to the Word of God than to all the thoughts of human beings and of angels. I will perform the duties of my office[88] and bring to light the facts in the case. As I have received the truth freely,[j] I will impart it without malice. For the rest let all look to their own salvation; I will do my part faithfully so that none may be able to cast on me the blame for their lack of faith and their ignorance of the truth when we appear before the judgment seat of Christ.[k]

In the first place, in order that we might safely and happily attain to a true and free knowledge of this sacrament, we must be particularly careful to put aside whatever has been added to

j   Matt. 10:8.
k   2 Cor. 5:10.

its original simple institution by human zeal and devotion: such things as vestments, ornaments, chants, prayers, organs, candles, and the whole pageantry of outward things. We must turn our eyes and hearts simply to the institution of Christ and this alone,[89] and set nothing before us but the very word of Christ by which he instituted the sacrament, made it perfect, and committed it to us. For in that word, and in that word alone, reside the power, the nature, and the whole substance of the Mass. All the rest is the work of human beings, added to the word of Christ, and the Mass can be held and remain a Mass just as well without them. Now the words of Christ, in which he instituted this sacrament, are these:

"Now as they were eating, Jesus took bread, and blessed, and broke it, and gave it to his disciples and said, 'Take, eat; this is my body, which is given for you.' And he took a cup, and when he had given thanks he gave it to them, saying, 'Drink of it, all of you; for this cup is the new testament in my blood, which is poured out for you and for many for the forgiveness of sins. Do this in remembrance of me.'"[90]

Albrecht Dürer's woodcut illustration
of the Lord's Supper (completed 1510).

87. Medieval church architecture facilitated these sacramental practices, from high altars for feast-day Masses to side altars and apsidiole chapels for private Masses, alcoves for the reservation and adoration of consecrated hosts, and screens dividing celebrants from the congregation.

88. As a sworn doctor of Holy Scripture (1512), Luther vowed to uphold the teachings of the Scripture and defend the faith from false doctrine.

89. Luther's examination of the biblical words of institution as the primary interpretation of the sacrament's meaning, benefit, and practice was first set forth a few months earlier in his *Treatise on the New Testament* (1520), LW 35:79–112.

90. Luther follows the canon of the Mass in conflating the various accounts of the words of institution from Matt. 26:26-28; Mark 14:22-24; Luke 22:19-20; and 1 Cor. 11:23-25, but excludes ornamental phrases in the canon not found explicitly in Scripture.

91. The Scholastic notion of the sacrament as an *opus operatum* is the doctrine that the priestly act intrinsically offers grace without reference to the disposition or faith of the recipient. Luther first challenges this understanding of the sacrament's efficacy in his *Sermon on the Blessed Sacrament of the Holy and True Body and Blood of Christ* (1519), LW 35:45–74; TAL 1:225–56.

92. Luther still held the traditional view that Paul was the author of the epistle to the Hebrews. He would change his mind on this by the time of his 1522 translation of the New Testament so that his preface to the epistle reads: ". . . Hebrews is not an epistle of St. Paul, or any other apostle . . . who wrote it is not known, and will probably not be known for a while; it makes no difference." He was probably influenced by Erasmus, who first questioned the Pauline authorship in his annotations to the New Testament. Earlier that year, in a sermon on Heb. 1:1-4, Luther suggested that Apollos might be the actual author.

These words the Apostle also delivers and more fully expounds in 1 Cor. 11[:23-26]. On them we must rest; on them we must build as on a firm rock, if we would not be carried about with every wind of doctrine,[l] as we have till now been carried about by the wicked doctrines of men who reject the truth.[m] For in these words nothing is omitted that pertains to the completeness, the use, and the blessing of this sacrament; and nothing is included that is superfluous and not necessary for us to know. Whoever sets aside these words and meditates or teaches concerning the Mass will teach monstrous and wicked doctrines, as they have done who have made of the sacrament an *opus operatum*[91] and a sacrifice.

Let this stand, therefore, as our first and infallible proposition—the Mass or Sacrament of the Altar is Christ's testament, which he left behind him at his death to be distributed among his believers. For that is the meaning of his words, "This cup is the new testament in my blood" [Luke 22:20; 1 Cor. 11:25]. Let this truth stand, I say, as the immovable foundation on which we shall base all that we have to say. For, as you will see, we are going to overthrow all the godless opinions of men which have been imported into this most precious sacrament. Christ, who is the truth, truly says that this is the new testament in his blood, poured out for us. Not without reason do I dwell on this sentence; the matter is of no small moment, and must be most deeply impressed on our minds.

Thus, if we enquire what a testament is, we shall learn at the same time what the Mass is, what its right use and blessing, and what its wrong use.

A testament, as everyone knows, is a promise made by one about to die, in which he designates his bequest and appoints his heirs. A testament, therefore, involves first, the death of the testator, and second, the promise of an inheritance and the naming of the heir. Thus Paul discusses at length the nature of a testament in Rom. 4[:13f.], Gal. 3[:15-17] and 4[:1-7], and Heb. 9[:15-18].[92] We see the same thing clearly also in these words of Christ. Christ testifies concerning his death when he says: "This is my body, which is given, this is my blood, which is poured out" [Luke 22:19-20]. He names and designates the bequest when he

l   Eph. 4:14.

m   Titus 1:14.

says "for the forgiveness of sins" [Matt. 26:28]. But he appoints the heirs when he says, "For you [Luke 22:19-20; 1 Cor. 11:24] and for many" [Matt. 26:28; Mark 14:24], that is, for those who accept and believe the promise of the testator. For here it is faith that makes us heirs, as we shall see.

You see, therefore, that what we call the Mass is a promise of the forgiveness of sins made to us by God, and such a promise as has been confirmed by the death of the Son of God. For the only difference between a promise and a testament is that the testament involves the death of the one who makes it. A testator is a promiser who is about to die, while a promiser (if I may put it thus) is a testator who is not about to die. This testament of Christ is foreshadowed in all the promises of God from the beginning of the world; indeed, whatever value those ancient promises possessed was altogether derived from this new promise that was to come in Christ. Hence the words "compact," "covenant," and "testament of the Lord"[93] occur so frequently in the Scriptures. These words signified that God would one day die. "For where there is a testament, the death of the testator must of necessity occur" (Heb. 9[:16]). Now God made a testament; therefore, it was necessary that God should die. But God could not die unless God became human. Thus the incarnation and the death of Christ are both comprehended most concisely in this one word, "testament."

From the above it will at once be seen what is the right and what is the wrong use of the Mass, and what is the worthy and what the unworthy preparation for it. If the Mass is a promise, as has been said, then access to it is to be gained, not with any works, or powers, or merits of one's own, but by faith alone. For where there is the word of the promising God, there must necessarily be the faith of the accepting person. It is plain, therefore, that the beginning of our salvation is a faith which clings to the word of the promising God, who, without any effort on our part, in free and unmerited mercy takes the initiative and offers us the word of his promise. "He sent forth his Word, and thus healed them," not: "He accepted our work, and thus healed us."[94] First of all there is God's Word. After it follows faith; after faith, love; then love does every good work, for it does no wrong; indeed, it is the fulfilling of the law.[95] In no other way can a person come to God or deal with God than through faith. That is to say, that the author of salvation is not human beings, by any works of their

93. The Latin for these three words are, respectively: *pactum, foedus, testamentum*. All three words are used interchangeably in the Latin Vulgate to translate the Hebrew *berith* in the Old Testament and the Greek *diathēkē* in the Septuagint or New Testament, rendered by most English translations as "covenant." E.g., Exod. 24:8: "Moses took the blood and dashed it on the people, and said, 'See the blood of the covenant [*sanguis foederis*] that the Lord has made with you in accordance with all these words'"; Gen. 9:8-9: "Then God said to Noah and to his sons with him, 'As for me, I am establishing my covenant [*pactum meum*] with you and your descendants after you . . .'"; Ps. 25:10: "All the paths of the LORD are steadfast love and faithfulness, for those who keep his covenant [*testamentum eius*] and his decrees."

94. Ps. 107:20. Luther inserted "thus" (*sic*) in his interpretation of the verse.

95. Rom. 13:10: "Love does no wrong to a neighbor; therefore love is the fulfilling of the law."

96. Heb. 1:3: "He is the radiance of the glory of God and the exact imprint of his nature, and he upholds the universe by the word of his power."

97. James 1:8: "Of his own will he brought us forth by the word of truth, that we should be a kind of firstfruits of his creatures."

98. Luther's reference to "hell" (*inferno*) here corresponds to the concept of *hades* or the Hebrew *Sheol* and the notion that, before Christ, the patriarchs remained imprisoned in this place of the dead until he would release them after his resurrection. Ephesians 4:7-10 and 1 Peter 3:19-20 were often interpreted as biblical allusions to this, and the view was relatively common in the early church. The medieval view was deeply influenced by the detailed account in the fourth-century apocryphal text *The Gospel of Nicodemus*. Dante (1265–1321) refers to this as the first circle of hell or "limbo." There the patriarchs of old were held until the "Mighty One," i.e., Christ, came and released them; cf. *Inferno*, Canto 4.52–63.

99. Hippolytus of Rome (170–235) referred to the place of the Old Testament righteous souls as the "Bosom of Abraham."

own," but God, through his promise; and that all things depend on, and are upheld and preserved by, the word of his power,[96] through which he brought us forth, to be a kind of first fruits of his creatures.[97]

Thus, in order to raise up Adam after the fall, God gave him this promise when he said to the serpent: "I will put enmity between you and the woman, and between your seed and her seed; he shall bruise your head, and you shall bruise his heel" [Gen. 3:15]. In this word of promise Adam, together with his descendants, was carried as it were in God's bosom, and by faith in it he was preserved, waiting patiently for the woman who should bruise the serpent's head, as God had promised. And in that faith and expectation he died, not knowing when or who she would be, yet never doubting that she would come. For such a promise, being the truth of God, preserves even in hell[98] those who believe it and wait for it. After this came another promise, made to Noah—to last until the time of Abraham—when a bow was set in the clouds as a sign of the covenant,*o* by faith in which Noah and his descendants found God gracious. After that, he promised Abraham that all the nations should be blessed in his seed.*p* And this is Abraham's bosom,*q* into which his descendants have been received.[99] Then to Moses and the children of Israel,*r* especially to David,*s* he gave the plainest promise of Christ, and thereby at last made clear what the promise to the people of old really was.

And so it finally came to the most perfect promise of all, that of the new testament, in which, with plain words, life and salvation are freely promised, and actually granted to those who believe the promise. And he distinguishes this testament from the old one by a particular mark when he calls it the "new testament." For the old testament given through Moses was not a promise of forgiveness of sins or of eternal things, but of temporal things, namely, of the land of Canaan, by which no one was renewed in spirit to lay hold on the heavenly inheritance.

n   The original here is singular.

o   Gen. 9:12-17.

p   Gen. 22:18.

q   Luke 16:22.

r   Deut. 18:18.

s   2 Sam. 7:12-16.

Wherefore also it was necessary that, as a figure of Christ, a dumb beast should be slain, in whose blood the same testament might be confirmed, as the blood corresponded to the testament and the sacrifice corresponded to the promise. But here Christ says "the new testament in my blood" [Luke 22:20; 1 Cor. 11:25], not somebody else's, but his own, by which grace is promised through the Spirit for the forgiveness of sins, that we may obtain the inheritance.

According to its substance, therefore, the Mass is nothing but the aforesaid words of Christ: "Take and eat, etc." [Matt. 26:26], as if he were saying: "Behold, O sinful and condemned human, out of the pure and unmerited love with which I love you, and by the will of the Father of mercies,[t] apart from any merit or desire of yours, I promise you in these words the forgiveness of all your sins and life everlasting. And that you may be absolutely certain of this irrevocable promise of mine, I shall give my body and pour out my blood, confirming this promise by my very death, and leaving you my body and blood as a sign and memorial of this same promise. As often as you partake of them, remember me, proclaim and praise my love and bounty toward you, and give thanks."

From this you will see that nothing else is needed for a worthy holding of Mass than a faith that relies confidently on this promise, believes Christ to be true in these words of his, and does not doubt that these infinite blessings have been bestowed upon it. Hard on this faith there follows, of itself, a most sweet stirring of the heart, whereby the human spirit is enlarged and enriched (that is love, given by the Holy Spirit through faith in Christ), so that a person is drawn to Christ, that gracious and bounteous testator, and made a thoroughly new and different person. Who would not shed tears of gladness, indeed, almost faint for joy in Christ, if he believed with unshaken faith that this inestimable promise of Christ belonged to him? How could he not help loving so great a benefactor, who of his own accord offers, promises, and grants such great riches and this eternal inheritance to one who is unworthy and deserving of something far different?

Therefore it is our one and only misfortune that we have many Masses in the world, and yet none, or very few of us, recognize, consider, and receive these promises and riches that are

t   2 Cor. 1:3.

offered to us. Actually, during the Mass, we should do nothing with greater zeal (indeed, it demands all our zeal) than to set before our eyes, meditate upon, and ponder these words, these promises of Christ—for they truly constitute the Mass itself—in order to exercise, nourish, increase, and strengthen our faith in them by this daily remembrance. For this is what he commands, when he says: "Do this in remembrance of me" [Luke 22:19; 1 Cor. 11:24]. This should be done by the preachers of the gospel in order to impress this promise faithfully upon the people, to commend it to them, and to awaken their faith in it.

But how many are there today who know that the Mass is the promise of Christ? I will say nothing of those godless preachers of fables, who teach human ordinances instead of this great promise. And even if they teach these words of Christ, they do not teach them as a promise or testament, neither therefore as a means of obtaining faith.

What we deplore in this captivity is that nowadays they take every precaution that no layperson should hear these words of Christ, as if they were too sacred to be delivered to the common people. So mad are we priests that we arrogate to ourselves alone the so-called words of consecration, to be said secretly,[100] yet in such a way that they do not profit even us, for we too fail to regard them as promises or as a testament for the strengthening of the faith. Instead of believing them, we reverence them with I know not what superstitious and godless fancies. What else is Satan trying to do to us through this misfortune of ours but to let nothing of the Mass remain in the church, though he is meanwhile at work filling every corner of the globe with Masses, that is, with abuses and mockeries of God's testament—burdening the world more and more heavily with most grievous sins of idolatry, to its deeper condemnation?[101] For what more sinful idolatry can there be than to abuse God's promises with perverse opinions and to neglect or extinguish faith in them?

For God does not deal, nor has God ever dealt, with people otherwise than through a word of promise, as I have said. We in turn cannot deal with God otherwise than through faith in the Word of his promise. God does not desire works, nor has God need of them; rather we deal with other people and with ourselves on the basis of works. But God has need of this: that we consider God faithful in God's promises,[102] and patiently persist in this belief, and thus worship God with faith, hope, and love.

---

100. In the early Middle Ages, softly spoken prayers, called *secreta*, occurred before the canon of the Mass (see also n. 170 below) because the offertory psalm was being sung by the choir simultaneously. Later (probably around the eighth century), the canon of the Mass began also to be prayed quietly, after the singing of the Preface and *Sanctus*. The reason for this is probably a combination of priestly piety and a pastoral concern for profane usage by the common people. Cf. Durandus, *Rationale divinorum officiorum* 4, 35, 2. Luther attacked this practice of the *Stillmesse* in a later treatise, *The Abomination of the Secret Mass* (1525), LW 36:311–28.

101. Luther means here that nothing remains in the church of the Mass as it should be understood and celebrated, even as more and more Masses are celebrated in the wrong way and for the wrong purpose.

102. Heb. 10:23: "Let us hold fast to the confession of our hope without wavering, for he who has promised is faithful."

It is in this way that God obtains glory among us, since it is not of ourselves who run, but of God who shows mercy, promises, and gives, that we have and hold all good things.[103] Behold, this is that true worship and service of God which we ought to perform in the Mass. But if the words of promise are not delivered, what exercise of faith can there be? And without faith, who can have hope or love? Without faith, hope, and love, what service of God can there be? There is no doubt, therefore, that in our day all priests and monks, together with their bishops and all their superiors, are idolators, living in a most perilous state by reason of this ignorance, abuse, and mockery of the Mass, or sacrament, or promise of God.

For anyone can easily see that these two, promise and faith, must necessarily go together. For without the promise there is nothing to be believed; while without faith the promise is useless, since it is established and fulfilled through faith. From this everyone will readily gather that the Mass, since it is nothing but promise, can be approached and observed only in faith. Without this faith, whatever else is brought to it by way of prayers, preparations, works, signs, or gestures are incitements to impiety rather than exercises of piety. It usually happens that those who are thus prepared imagine themselves legitimately entitled to approach the altar, when in reality they are less prepared than at any other time or by any other work, by reason of the unbelief which they bring with them. How many celebrants you can see everywhere, every day, who imagine they—wretched men—have committed criminal offenses when they make some petty mistake, such as wearing the wrong vestment, or forgetting to wash their hands, or stumbling over their prayers! But the fact that they have no regard for or faith in the Mass itself, namely, the divine promise, causes them not the slightest qualms of conscience. O worthless religion of this age of ours, the most godless and thankless of all ages!

Hence the only worthy preparation and proper observance is faith, the faith by which we believe in the Mass, that is, in the divine promise. Those, therefore, who desire to approach the altar or receive the sacrament, let them beware lest they appear empty-handed before the face of the Lord God.[104] But they will be empty-handed unless they have faith in the Mass, or this new testament. By what godless work could they sin more grievously against the truth of God, than by this unbelief of theirs? By it,

103. Rom. 9:16: "So it depends not on human will or exertion, but on God who shows mercy."

104. Cf. Exod. 23:15: "You shall observe the festival of unleavened bread. . . . No one shall appear before me empty-handed"; Deut. 16:16: "Three times a year all your males shall appear before the Lord your God at the place that he will choose: at the festival of unleavened bread, at the festival of weeks, and at the festival of booths. They shall not appear before the Lord empty-handed."

105. This definition of unbelief can be found consistently through the earliest writings of Luther, especially as it touches on Rom. 3:4 and its citation of Pss. 116:11 and 51:4, "Although everyone is a liar, let God be proved true, as it is written, 'So that you may be justified in your words, and prevail in your judging.'"

106. Perhaps a reference to the consequences of unworthy eating that Paul mentions in 1 Cor. 11:29.

107. Luther gives many of the same examples in his earlier *Treatise on the New Testament* (1520), LW 35:86.

as much as in their lies, they convict God of being a liar and a maker of empty promises.[105,u] The safest course, therefore, will be to go to the Mass in the same spirit in which you would go to hear any other promise of God, that is, prepared not to do or contribute much yourself, but to believe and accept all that is promised you there, or proclaimed as promises through the ministry of the priest. If you do not come in this spirit, beware of attending at all, for you will surely be going to your judgment.[106]

I was right then in saying that the whole power of the Mass consists in the words of Christ, in which he testifies that forgiveness of sins is bestowed on all those who believe that his body is given and his blood poured out for them. This is why nothing is more important for those who go to hear Mass than to ponder these words diligently and in full faith. Unless they do this, all else that they do is in vain. This is surely true, that to every promise of his, God usually adds some sign as a memorial or remembrance of the promise, so that thereby we may serve him the more diligently and he may admonish us the more effectually.[107] Thus, when he promised Noah that he would not again destroy the world by a flood, he added his bow in the clouds, to show that he would be mindful of his covenant [Gen. 9:8-17]. And after promising Abraham the inheritance in his seed, he gave him circumcision as a mark of his justification by faith [Gen. 17:3-11]. Thus he granted to Gideon the dry and the wet fleece to confirm his promise of victory over the Midianites [Judg. 6:36-40]. And through Isaiah he offered to Ahaz a sign that he would conquer the king of Syria and Samaria, to confirm in him his faith in the promise [Isa. 7:10-17]. And we read of many such signs of the promises of God in the Scriptures.

So in the Mass also, the foremost promise of all, he adds as a memorial sign of such a great promise his own body and his own blood in the bread and wine, when he says: "Do this in remembrance of me" [Luke 22:19; 1 Cor. 11:24-25]. And so in baptism, to the words of promise he adds the sign of immersion in water. We may learn from this that in every promise of God two things are presented to us, the word and the sign, so that we are to understand the word to be the testament, but the sign to be the sacrament. Thus, in the Mass, the word of Christ is the testament, and the bread and wine are the sacrament. And as

u   The original of these sentences is singular.

there is greater power in the word than in the sign, so there is greater power in the testament than in the sacrament; for a man can have and use the word or testament apart from the sign or sacrament. "Believe," says Augustine, "and you have eaten."[v] But what does one believe, other than the word of the one who promises? Therefore I can hold Mass every day, indeed, every hour, for I can set the words of Christ before me and with them feed and strengthen my faith as often as I choose. This is a truly spiritual eating and drinking.[108]

Here you may see what great things our theologians of the *Sentences*[109] have produced in this matter. In the first place, not one of them treats of that which is first and foremost, namely, the testament and the word of promise. And thus they make us forget faith and the whole power of the Mass. In addition, they discuss exclusively the second part of the Mass, namely, the sign or sacrament; yet in such a way that here too they do not teach faith, but their preparations and *opera operata*,[w] participations[x] and fruits of the Mass.[110] They come then to the profundities, babble of transubstantiation, and endless other metaphysical trivialities, destroy the proper understanding and use of both sacrament and testament together with faith as such, and cause Christ's people to forget their God—as the prophet says, days without number [Jer. 2:32]. Let the others tabulate the various benefits of hearing Mass; you just apply your mind to this, that you may say and believe with the prophet that God has here prepared a table before you in the presence of your enemies [Ps. 23:5], at which your faith may feed and grow fat. But your faith is fed only with the word of divine promise, for "One does not live by bread alone, but by every word that proceeds from the mouth of God" [Deut. 8:3; Matt. 4:4]. Hence, in the Mass you must pay closest heed above all to the word of promise, as to a most lavish banquet—your utterly green pastures and sacred still waters [Ps. 23:2]—in order that you might esteem this word above everything else, trust in it supremely, and cling to it most firmly, even through death and all sins. If you do this, you will obtain not merely those tiny drops and crumbs of "fruits of the

108. For a Scholastic understanding of spiritual eating in the sacrament, cf. Aquinas, *STh* III, q. 80, a. 2: "there are two ways of eating spiritually. First, . . . the angels eat Christ spiritually inasmuch as they are united with Him in the enjoyment of perfect charity, and in clear vision. . . . In another way one may eat Christ spiritually, . . . as a man believes in Christ, while desiring to receive this sacrament."

109. That is, commentators on the *Sentences* of Peter Lombard. See n. 56, p. 30.

110. "Fruits of the Mass" (*fructus missae*) has to do with the character and extent of benefits received in the celebration of the Mass, especially the relationship between the infinite benefits procured by Christ and present *ex opere operato* and the limited benefits correlative to the intensity of the devotion of those who participate.

v   Cf. Augustine, *Sermo* 112, 5.

w   See n. 91, p. 40.

x   See n. 83, p. 38.

Mass" which some have superstitiously invented, but the very fountainhead of life, namely, that faith in the Word out of which every good thing flows, as is said in John 4:[111] "He who believes in me, 'Out of his heart shall flow rivers of living water.'" And again, "Whoever drinks of the water that I shall give him, it will become in him a spring of water welling up to eternal life" [John 4:14].

Now there are two things that are constantly assailing us, so that we fail to gather the fruits of the Mass. The first is that we are sinners, and unworthy of such great things because of our utter worthlessness. The second is that, even if we were worthy, these things are so high that our timid nature does not dare to aspire to them or hope for them. For who would not simply stand awe-struck before the forgiveness of sins and life everlasting rather than seek after them, once he had weighed properly the magnitude of the blessings which come through them, namely, to have God as father, to be God's child and heir of all God's goods! Against this twofold timidity of ours we must lay hold on the word of Christ, and fix our gaze much more steadfastly on it than on these thoughts of our own weakness. For "great are the works of the Lord, studied by all who have pleasure in them" [Ps. 111:2], who is able to give "more abundantly than all that we ask or think" [Eph. 3:20]. If they did not surpass our worthiness, our grasp, and all our thoughts, they would not be divine. Thus Christ also encourages us when he says: "Fear not, little flock, for it is your Father's good pleasure to give you the kingdom" [Luke 12:32]. For it is just this incomprehensible overflowing of God's goodness, showered upon us through Christ, that moves us above all to love God most ardently in return, to be drawn to God with fullest confidence, and, despising all else, be ready to suffer all things for God. Wherefore this sacrament is rightly called "a fountain of love."[112]

Let us take an illustration of this from human experience.[113] If a very rich lord were to bequeath a thousand gold coins[114] to a beggar or to an unworthy and wicked servant, it is certain that he would boldly claim and accept them without regard to his unworthiness and the greatness of the bequest. And if anyone should seek to oppose him on the grounds of his unworthiness and the large amount of the legacy, what do you suppose the man would say? He would likely say: "What is that to you? What I accept, I accept not on my merits or by any right that I may personally have to it. I know that I am receiving more than

---

111. John 7:38. Luther was looking ahead to the next verse cited from John 4.

112. While the phrase "fount of love" (*fons dilectionis*) is more commonly applied to the Blessed Virgin Mary in the Middle Ages, love is clearly the central benefit of the sacrament according to Scholastic theology, yet in such a way that love is infused in the recipient as a virtue meriting divine favor. See, for example, Lombard, *Sentences* 4, d. 12, c. 6: "For this Sacrament was instituted for two reasons: for the increase of virtue, namely love, and as medicine for our daily infirmity."

113. Luther used the following illustration in his earlier *Treatise on the New Testament* (1520), LW 35:89f.

114. *Guldens,* gold coins of the time, perhaps of the Holy Roman Empire.

a worthless one like me deserves; indeed, I have deserved the very opposite. But I claim what I claim by the right of a bequest and of another's goodness. If to Christ it was not an unworthy thing to bequeath so great a sum to an unworthy person, why should I refuse to accept it because of my unworthiness? Indeed, it is for this very reason that I cherish all the more his unmerited gift—because I am unworthy!" With that same thought all people[y] ought to fortify their consciences against all qualms and scruples, so that they may lay hold on the promise of Christ with unwavering faith, and take the greatest care to approach the sacrament not trusting in confession, prayer, and preparation, but rather, despairing of all these, with firm confidence in Christ who gives the promise. For, as we have said often enough, the word of promise must reign alone here in pure faith; such faith is the one and only sufficient preparation.

Hence we see how great is God's wrath with us, in that God has permitted godless teachers to conceal the words of this testament from us, and thereby to extinguish this same faith, as far as they could. It is already easy to see what is the inevitable result of this extinguishing of the faith, namely, the most godless superstition of works. For where faith dies and the word of faith is silent, there works and the prescribing of works immediately crowd into their place. By them we have been carried away out of our own land, as into a Babylonian captivity, and despoiled of all our precious possessions. This has been the fate of the Mass; it has been converted by the teaching of godless people into a good work. They themselves call it an *opus operatum*,[z] and by it they presume themselves to be all-powerful with God. Next they proceed to the very height of madness, and after inventing the lie that the Mass is effective simply by virtue of the act having been performed, they add another one to the effect that the Mass is none the less profitable to others even if it is harmful to some wicked priest who may be celebrating it.[115] On such a foundation of sand they base their applications, participations, brotherhoods, anniversaries,[a] and numberless other lucrative and profitable schemes of that kind.

115. Cf. Aquinas, *STh* III, q. 82, a. 6: "By reason of the power of the Holy Spirit, who communicates to each one the blessings of Christ's members on account of their being united in charity, the private blessing in the Mass of a good priest is fruitful to others. But the private evil of one man cannot hurt another, except the latter, in some way, consent." Luther refers here to the prayers of the Mass as an offering to God and not to the sacrament itself, which is God's work regardless of the worthiness of the priest. See below, p. 59.

y   This sentence is singular in the original.

z   See n. 91, p. 40.

a   See n. 82, 83, and 85, p. 38.

These fraudulent disguises are so powerful, so numerous, and so firmly entrenched that you can scarcely prevail against them unless you exercise unremitting care and bear well in mind what the Mass is and what has been said above. You have seen that the Mass is nothing else than the divine promise or testament of Christ, sealed with the sacrament of his body and blood. If that is true, you will understand that it cannot possibly be in any way a work; nobody can possibly do any thing in it, neither can it be dealt with in any other way than by faith alone. However, faith is not a work, but the lord and life of all works.[b] Who in the world is so foolish as to regard a promise received by him, or a testament given to him, as a good work, which he renders to the testator by his acceptance of it? What heir will imagine that he is doing his departed father a kindness by accepting the terms of the will and the inheritance it bequeaths to him? What godless audacity is it, therefore, when we who are to receive the testament of God come as those who would perform a good work for God! This ignorance of the testament, this captivity of so great a sacrament—are they not too sad for tears? When we ought to be grateful for benefits received, we come arrogantly to give that which we ought to take. With unheard-of perversity we mock the mercy of the giver by giving as a work the thing we receive as a gift, so that the testator, instead of being a dispenser of his own goods, becomes the recipient of ours. Woe to such sacrilege!

Who has ever been so mad as to regard baptism as a good work, or what candidate for baptism has believed that he was performing a work which he might offer to God on behalf of himself and communicate to others? If, then, there is no good work that can be communicated to others in this one sacrament and testament, neither will there be any in the Mass, since it too is nothing else than a testament and sacrament. Hence it is a manifest and wicked error to offer or apply the Mass for sins, for satisfactions, for the dead, or for any needs whatsoever of one's own or of others.[116] You will readily see the obvious truth of this if you firmly hold that the Mass is a divine promise, which can benefit no one, be applied to no one, intercede for no one, and be communicated to no one, except only to one who believes with a

116. Luther is speaking against the so-called votive Mass, a Mass said with an intention other than the usual celebration of the day's divine office—often as an intercession for the sake of some need, e.g., the sick, the dead, the penitent, etc. It was a common practice throughout the Middle Ages, and became increasingly common due to the acceptance of money in exchange for such a Mass.

b   On the relationship between faith and works, see Luther's *Treatise on Good Works* (1520), LW 44:15–114; TAL 1:257–368.

faith of one's own. Who can receive or apply, in behalf of another, the promise of God, which demands the personal faith of each one individually? Can I give to another the promise of God, even if that person does not believe? Can I believe for another, or cause another to believe? But this is what must happen if I am able to apply and communicate the Mass to others; for there are but two things in the Mass, the divine promise and the human faith, the latter accepting what the former promises. But if it is true that I can do this, then I can also hear and believe the gospel for another, I can be baptized for another, I can be absolved from sins for another, I can also partake of the Sacrament of the Altar for another, and—to go through the list of their sacraments also—I can marry a wife for another, get ordained for another, be confirmed for another, and receive extreme unction for another!

In short, why did not Abraham believe for all the Jews? Why was faith in the promise made to Abraham demanded of every individual Jew?[c]

Therefore, let this irrefutable truth stand fast: Where there is a divine promise, there everyone must stand on his own feet; his own personal faith is demanded, he will give an account for himself and bear his own load;[d] as it is said in the last chapter of Mark [16:16]: "He who believes and is baptized will be saved; but he who does not believe will be condemned." Even so each one can derive personal benefit from the Mass only by one's own personal faith. It is absolutely impossible to commune on behalf of anyone else. Just as the priest is unable to administer the sacrament to anyone on behalf of another, but administers the same sacrament to each one individually by himself. For in consecrating and administering, the priests are our servants. Through them we are not offering a good work or communicating something in an active sense. Rather, we are receiving through them the promises and the sign; we are being communicated unto in the passive sense. This is the view that has persisted with respect to the laity right up to the present day, for of them it is said not that they do something good but that they receive it. But the priests have strayed into godless ways; out of the sacrament and testament of God, which ought to be a good gift received, they

c   Cf. Gen. 12:1f.; 15:5f.
d   Gal. 6:5.

have made for themselves a good deed performed, which they then give to others and offer up to God.

But you will say: What is this? Will you not overturn the practice and teaching of all the churches and monasteries, by virtue of which they have flourished all these centuries? For the Mass is the foundation of their anniversaries, intercessions, applications, communications, etc., that is to say, of their fat income. I answer: This is the very thing that has constrained me to write of the captivity of the church.[117] For it is in this manner that the sacred testament of God has been forced into the service of a most impious traffic. It has come through the opinions and ordinances of wicked men, who, passing over the Word of God, have dished up to us the thoughts of their own hearts and led the whole world astray. What do I care about the number and influence of those who are in this error? The truth is mightier than all of them. If you are able to refute Christ, who teaches that the Mass is a testament and a sacrament, then I will admit that they are in the right. Or, if you can bring yourself to say that that man is doing a good work who receives the benefit of the testament, or to that end uses this sacrament of promise, then I will gladly condemn my teachings. But since you can do neither, why do you hesitate to turn your back on the multitude who go after evil? Why do you hesitate to give God the glory and to confess God's truth—that all priests today are perversely mistaken who regard the Mass as a work by which they may relieve their own needs and those of others, whether dead or alive? I am uttering unheard of and startling things, but if you will consider what the Mass is, you will realize that I have spoken the truth. The fault lies with our false sense of security, which blinds us to the wrath of God that is raging against us.

I am ready to admit, however, that the prayers which we pour out before God when we are gathered together to partake of the Mass are good works or benefits, which we impart, apply, and communicate to one another, and which we offer for one another.[118] Thus James [5:16] teaches us to pray for one another that we may be healed, and Paul in 1 Tim. 2[:1-2] commands "that supplications, prayers, and intercessions be made for all men, for kings and all who are in high positions." Now these are not the Mass, but works of the Mass—if the prayers of heart and lips may be called works—for they flow from the faith that is kindled or increased in the sacrament. For the Mass, or the

117. The transposition of the divine generosity and promise of the sacrament into a human work, the justification of this practice by human opinion and tradition rather than the Scriptures, and the consequent enlargement of papal power and riches are, for Luther, the fundamental abuses of the church. Much of his early theological critique can be summarized here: (1) the gospel is not to be turned into a law; (2) the word of God is the final theological authority, not human opinion; and (3) the church should shepherd the flock with practices and doctrine that strengthen faith in Christ, not fleece the sheep for its own gain.

118. In his early writings (e.g., *First Lectures on the Psalms*, 1513–1515), Luther can talk about the Mass as a sacrifice but limits the language to sacrifices of praise and thanksgiving (*sacrificium confessionis . . . laudis*). In his 1520 *Treatise on the New Testament*, Luther further develops this line of interpretation for the eucharistic sacrifice: "To be sure

promise of God, is not fulfilled by praying, but only by believing. However, as believers we pray and perform every good work. But what priest offers up the sacrifice in this sense, that he believes he is offering up only the prayers? They all imagine that they are offering up Christ himself to God the Father as an all-sufficient sacrifice, and performing a good work for all those whom they intend to benefit, for they put their trust in the work which the Mass accomplishes, and they do not ascribe this work to prayer. In this way the error has gradually grown, until they have come to ascribe to the sacrament what belongs to the prayers, and to offer to God what should be received as a benefit.

We must therefore sharply distinguish the testament and sacrament itself from the prayers that we offer at the same time. Not only this, but we must also bear in mind that the prayers avail utterly nothing, either to him who offers them or to those for whom they are offered, unless the testament is first received in faith, so that it will be faith that offers the prayers; for faith alone is heard, as James teaches in his first chapter.[119] There is therefore a great difference between prayer and the Mass. Prayer may be extended to as many persons as one desires, while the Mass is received only by the persons who believe for themselves, and only to the extent that they believe. It cannot be given either to God or to human beings. Rather it is God alone who through the ministration of the priest gives it to people, and people receive it by faith alone without any works or merits. Nor would anyone dare to be so foolish as to assert that a ragged beggar does a good work when he comes to receive a gift from a rich man. But the Mass (as I have said) is the gift of the divine promise, proffered to all people by the hand of the priest.

It is certain, therefore, that the Mass is not a work which may be communicated to others, but the object of faith (as has been said), for the strengthening and nourishing of each one's own faith.

Now there is yet a second stumbling block that must be removed, and this is much greater and the most dangerous of all. It is the common belief that the Mass is a sacrifice, which is offered to God. Even the words of the canon[120] seem to imply this, when they speak of "these gifts, these presents, these holy sacrifices," and further on "this offering." Prayer is also made, in so many words, "that the sacrifice may be accepted even as the sacrifice of Abel," etc. Hence Christ is termed "the sacrifice

this sacrifice of prayer, praise, and thanksgiving, and of ourselves as well, we are not to present before God in our own person. But we are to lay it upon Christ and let him present it for us as St. Paul teaches in Hebrews 13:15, 'Let us continually offer up a sacrifice of praise to God, that is, the fruit of lips that confess him and praise him,' and all this 'through Christ.' For this is why he is also a priest. . . . From these words we learn that we do not offer Christ as a sacrifice, but that Christ offers us. And in this way it is permissible, yea profitable, to call the Mass a sacrifice . . ." (LW 35:98–99).

119. James 1:5-8: "If any of you is lacking in wisdom, ask God, who gives to all generously and ungrudgingly, and it will be given you. But ask in faith, never doubting, for the one who doubts is like a wave of the sea, driven and tossed by the wind; for the doubter, being double-minded and unstable in every way, must not expect to receive anything from the Lord."

120. The canon of the Mass consisted of a series of prayers and collects that included the words of institution for the consecration of the bread and wine. In other words, the entire form of the liturgy around the consecration puts the celebration of the sacrament into the context of a priestly sacrifice and work spoken on behalf of the people, even as other prayers are such.

121. Luther's ironic use of the Scholastic language of transubstantiation is to illustrate that the papal Mass has focused on incidentals and ignored the essence or chief aspect of the sacrament.

122. The monstrance (from the Latin, *monstrare*, "to show") is a vessel designed to display the consecrated host for the veneration of the faithful, especially in the context of a liturgical procession like that of Palm Sunday or Corpus Christi. The practice of displaying and processing the consecrated host grew quickly out of the practice of the elevation of the host for the purpose of adoration. The elevation was introduced into the eucharistic liturgy in Paris in the thirteenth century, probably as a response to those who argued that the host was not the body of Christ until the wine was also consecrated. Evidence for the use of a monstrance can be identified from the fourteenth century.

123. Also called a "pall" (Lat. *palla*), which at the time was the cloth upon which the chalice and host rested. The corporal cloth was then often kept with the consecrated host.

of the altar." Added to these are the sayings of the holy fathers, the great number of examples, and the widespread practice uniformly observed throughout the world.

Over against all these things, firmly entrenched as they are, we must resolutely set the words and example of Christ. For unless we firmly hold that the Mass is the promise or testament of Christ, as the words clearly say, we shall lose the whole gospel and all its comfort. Let us permit nothing to prevail against these words—even though an angel from heaven should teach otherwise [Gal. 1:8]—for they contain nothing about a work or a sacrifice. Moreover, we also have the example of Christ on our side. When he instituted this sacrament and established this testament at the Last Supper, Christ did not offer himself to God the Father, nor did he perform a good work on behalf of others, but, sitting at the table, he set this same testament before each one and proffered to him the sign. Now, the more closely our Mass resembles that first Mass of all, which Christ performed at the Last Supper, the more Christian it will be. But Christ's Mass was most simple, without any display of vestments, gestures, chants, or other ceremonies, so that if it had been necessary to offer the Mass as a sacrifice, then Christ's institution of it was not complete.

Not that anyone should revile the church universal for embellishing and amplifying the Mass with many additional rites and ceremonies. But what we contend for is this: No one should be deceived by the glamor of the ceremonies and entangled in the multitude of pompous forms, and thus lose the simplicity of the Mass itself, and indeed practice a sort of transubstantiation by losing sight of the simple "substance" of the Mass and clinging to the manifold "accidents" of outward pomp.[121] For whatever has been added to the word and example of Christ is an "accident" of the Mass, and ought to be regarded just as we regard the so-called monstrances[122] and corporal cloths[123] in which the host itself is contained.

Therefore, just as distributing a testament or accepting a promise differs diametrically from offering a sacrifice, so it is a contradiction in terms to call the Mass a sacrifice, for the former is something that we receive and the latter is something that we give. The same thing cannot be received and offered at the same time, nor can it be both given and accepted by the same person, any more than our prayer can be the same thing as that which

In this sixteenth-century design for a monstrance by Daniel Hopfer (c. 1470–1535) the host is to be displayed in the center supported by angels. The twelve disciples occupy the niches above.

our prayer obtains, or the act of praying be the same thing as the act of receiving that for which we pray.

What shall we say then of the canon of the Mass and the patristic authorities? First of all, I would answer: If there were nothing at all to be said against them, it would be safer to reject them all than admit that the Mass is a work or a sacrifice, lest we deny the word of Christ and destroy faith together with the Mass. Nevertheless, in order to retain them, we shall say that we are instructed by the Apostle in 1 Cor. 11 that it was customary for Christ's believers, when they came together for Mass, to bring with them food and drink.[124] These they called "collections," and they distributed them among all who were in want, after the example of the apostles in Acts 4.[125] From this store was taken the portion of the bread and wine that was consecrated in

124. 1 Cor. 11:21, 33-34: "For when the time comes to eat, each of you goes ahead with your own supper, and one goes hungry and another becomes drunk. . . . So then, my brothers and sisters, when you come together to eat, wait for one another. If you are hungry, eat at home, so that when you come together, it will not be for your condemnation."

125. Acts 4:34-35: "There was not a needy person among them, for as many as owned lands or houses sold them and brought the proceeds of what was sold. They laid it at the apostles' feet, and it was distributed to each as any had need."

126. See, for example, Hippolytus, *The Apostolic Tradition*, chs. 5–6, where it speaks about the bringing of oil, olives, milk, and cheese in addition to the bread and wine that is consecrated.

127. 1 Tim. 4:4-5: "For everything created by God is good, and nothing is to be rejected, provided it is received with thanksgiving; for it is sanctified by God's word and by prayer."

128. Lev. 8:27: "He placed all these on the palms of Aaron and on the palms of his sons, and raised them as an elevation offering before the LORD."

129. Luther supposes that the history of the elevation of the host is connected to the language of the Old Testament offering, giving the origin of the practice the benefit of the doubt. However, see n. 133 below.

130. Isa. 37:4: "It may be that the LORD your God heard the words of the Rabshakeh, whom his master the king of Assyria has sent to mock the living God, and will rebuke the words that the LORD your God has heard; therefore lift up your prayer for the remnant that is left."

131. Philip Melanchthon (1497–1560) sets forth an argument similar to Luther's in the *Apology of the Augsburg Confession*, XXIV, BC, 258–277.

132. Referring to a holy presentation made to God. Here, the offering of bread and wine.

133. This is an example of Luther's conservative approach to reform. While he distinguishes sharply between the essence of the sacrament as it centers on the words of Christ from the ceremonies and prayers that surround this, Luther is still willing to retain

the sacrament.[126] And since all this store was consecrated by the word and prayer,[127] by being "lifted up" according to the Hebrew rite of which we read in Moses,[128] the words and rite of this lifting up or offering have come down to us, although the custom of bringing along and collecting that which was offered or lifted up has long since fallen into disuse.[129] Thus, in Isa. 37 Hezekiah commanded Isaiah to lift up his prayer in the sight of God for the remnant.[130] In the Psalms we read: "Lift up your hands to the holy place" [Ps. 134:2]. And again: "To you I will lift up my hands" [Ps. 63:4]. And in 1 Tim. 2[:8]: "In every place lifting holy hands." For this reason the words "sacrifice" and "offering" must be taken to refer not to the sacrament and testament, but to the collections themselves.[131] From this source also the word *collect* has come down to us for the prayers said in the Mass.

The same thing happens when the priest elevates the bread and the cup immediately after consecrating them. By this he does not show that he is offering anything to God, for he does not say a single word here about a victim or an offering. But this elevation is either a survival of that Hebrew rite of lifting up what was received with thanksgiving and returned to God, or else it is an admonition to us to provoke us to faith in this testament which the priest has set forth and exhibited in the words of Christ, so that now he also shows us the sign of the testament. Thus the oblation[132] of the bread properly accompanies the demonstrative "this" in the words, "this is my body," and by the sign the priest addresses us gathered about him; and in a like manner the oblation of the cup properly accompanies the demonstrative "this" in the words, "this cup is the new testament, etc." For it is faith that the priest ought to awaken in us by this act of elevation.[133] And would to God that as he elevates the sign, or sacrament, openly before our eyes, he might also sound in our ears the word, or testament, in a loud, clear voice, and in the language of the people,[134] whatever it may be, in order that faith may be the more effectively awakened. For why may Mass be said in Greek and Latin and Hebrew, but not in German or any other language?[e]

Therefore, let the priests who offer the sacrifice of the Mass in these corrupt and most perilous times take heed, first, that they do not refer to the sacrament the words of the greater and lesser canon,[135] together with the collects, because they smack

---

e   See on p. 130 an image of the cover of Luther's *Deutsche Messe*.

too strongly of sacrifice. They should refer them instead to the bread and the wine to be consecrated, or to their own prayers. For the bread and wine are offered beforehand for blessing in order that they may be sanctified by the word and by prayer,[f] but after they have been blessed and consecrated they are no longer offered, but received as a gift from God. And in this rite let the priest bear in mind that the gospel is to be set above all canons and collects devised by men, and that the gospel does not sanction the idea that the Mass is a sacrifice, as has been shown.

Further, when a priest celebrates public Mass, he should determine to do nothing else than to commune himself and others by means of the Mass. At the same time, however, he may offer prayers for himself and others, but he must beware lest he presume to offer the Mass. But let him that holds private Masses determine to commune himself.[136] The private Mass does not differ in the least from the ordinary communion which any person receives at the hand of the priest, and has no greater effect. The difference is in the prayers, and in the fact that the priest consecrates the elements for himself and administers them to himself. As far as the blessing of the Mass and sacrament is concerned we are all equals, whether we are priests or lay.

If a priest is requested by others to celebrate so-called votive Masses,[g] let him beware of accepting a fee for the Mass, or of presuming to offer any votive sacrifice. Rather, he should take pains to refer all this to the prayers which he offers for the dead or the living, saying to himself: "Lo, I will go and receive the sacrament for myself alone, and while doing so I will pray for this one and that one." Thus he will receive his fee for the prayers, not for the Mass, and can buy food and clothing with it.[137] Let him not be disturbed because all the world holds and practices the contrary. You have the utmost certainty of the gospel, and by relying on it, you may well disregard the belief and opinions of others. But if you disregard me and insist upon offering the Mass and not the prayers alone, remember that I have faithfully warned you, and that I will be without blame on the day of judgment; you will have to bear your sin alone.[h] I have said what I was bound to say to you as brother to brother for your salvation; yours will be

---

f   1 Tim. 4:5.

g   See n. 116, p. 50.

h   Cf. Ezek. 3:19; 33:9.

traditional rites as long as they support the original biblical intention of the sacrament, namely, to awaken faith in the gospel.

134. Luther's pastoral desire to have the Mass in the vernacular is realized in his later efforts at liturgical reform, especially in his *Deutsche Messe und Ordnung des Gottesdiensts—The German Mass and Order of Service* (1526), LW 53:51–90; also pp. 131–61 in this volume. He also reformed the Latin Mass along the lines indicated here so that the benefit of sacrament as testament rather than sacrifice is clear; see his *Formula missae et communionis pro ecclesia Vuittembergensi* (*An Order of Mass and Communion for the Church at Wittenberg*) (1523), LW 53:15–40.

135. The offering until the conclusion of the communion distribution was considered the "canon" of the Mass. However, a distinction was made between the prayers following the prefatory dialogue (e.g., *Sursum corda*), and then the prayers leading to consecration that followed the *Sanctus*, the former being the "lesser canon" (*canon minor*) and the latter, the "greater canon" (*canon maior*).

136. The private Mass (*missa privata*) was just as it sounds, a Mass celebrated by a priest without a congregation. Luther's concern here is that someone actually commune to make it clear that the Mass is not intended only as a sacrifice. He would later reject the practice altogether; see *The Misuse of the Mass* (1521), LW 36:127–230.

137. Again, Luther is quite conservative in his approach. Focusing solely on preserving the gracious character of the sacrament, Luther allows prayers for the dead and even the fees exacted to continue as long as they are distinguished from the Mass itself.

138. Gregory I, "the Great" (b. 540), was pope from 590 to 604.

139. This precise quotation from Gregory cannot be identified, but the idea that the efficacy of the Mass is not dependent on the piety of the priest is prominent since Augustine's writings against the Donatists. Cf. *Augsburg Confession*, VII, BC, 42–43.

140. While the Scholastic distinction of *opus operatum* and *opus operantis* may have been used to excuse wicked behavior, the original intention of the distinction was to differentiate between the efficacy of the sacraments of the Old Testament and that of the New. Since the sacrifices proscribed in the Mosiac law were merely signs pointing ahead to the death of Christ, their power to impart grace was not intrinsic but dependent on the faith and disposition of those performing the sacrifice (*opus operantis*). On the other hand, since the Eucharist was not a sign but the true sacrificial blood of Christ, its efficacy was intrinsic regardless of the faith or piety of the celebrant or recipient (*opus operatum*). See Artur Michael Landgraf, "Die Gnadenökonomie des Alten Bundes nach der Lehre der Frühscholastik," "Die Wirkungen der Beschneidung," and "Beiträge der Frühscholastik zur Terminologie der allgemeinen Sakramentenlehre," in *Dogmengeschichte der Frühscholastik*, 3/1 (Regensburg: Friedrich Pustet, 1954), 19–168.

the gain if you observe it, yours the loss if you neglect it. And if some should even condemn what I have said, I will reply in the words of Paul: "But evil men and impostors will go on from bad to worse, deceiving and being deceived" [2 Tim 3:13].

From the above everyone will readily understand the often quoted saying of Gregory:[138] "A Mass celebrated by a wicked priest is not to be considered of less effect than one celebrated by a good priest. Neither would a Mass of St. Peter have been better than that of Judas the traitor, if they had offered the sacrifice of the Mass."[139] This saying has served many as a cloak to cover their godless doings, and because of it they have invented the distinction between the *opus operatum* and the *opus operantis*, so as to be free to lead wicked lives themselves and yet benefit others.[140] Gregory speaks the truth, only they misunderstand his words. For it is true beyond a question that the testament or sacrament is given and received through the ministration of wicked priests no less completely than through the ministration of the most saintly. For who has any doubt that the gospel is preached by the ungodly? Now the Mass is part of the gospel; indeed, it is the sum and substance of it. For what is the whole gospel but the good tidings of the forgiveness of sins? Whatever can be said about forgiveness of sins and the mercy of God in the broadest and richest sense is all briefly comprehended in the word of this testament. For this reason popular sermons ought to be nothing else than expositions of the Mass, or explanations of the divine promise of this testament; this would be to teach the faith and truly to edify the church. But in our day the expounders of the Mass make mockery and jest with allegorical explanations of human ceremonies.

Therefore, just as a wicked priest may baptize, that is, apply the word of promise and the sign of water to the candidate for baptism, so he may also set forth the promise of this sacrament and administer it to those who partake, and even partake himself, as did Judas the traitor at the supper of the Lord.[i] It still remains the same sacrament and testament, which works its own work in the believer but an "alien work" in the unbeliever.[141] But when it comes to offering a sacrifice the case is quite different. For not the Mass but the prayers are offered to God, and therefore it is as plain as day that the offerings of a wicked priest avail

i   Matt. 26:23-25.

nothing, but, as Gregory says again: When an unworthy person is sent as the intercessor, the heart of the judge is only turned to greater disfavor.[142] Therefore these two things—Mass and prayer, sacrament and work, testament and sacrifice—must not be confused; for the one comes from God to us through the ministration of the priest and demands our faith, the other proceeds from our faith to God through the priest and demands his hearing. The former descends, the latter ascends. The former, therefore, does not necessarily require a worthy and godly minister, but the latter does indeed require such a one, for "God does not listen to sinners" [John 9:31]. He knows how to do good through evil people, but he does not accept the work of any evil person; as he showed in the case of Cain,[143] and as is said in Prov. 15[:8]: "The sacrifice of the wicked is an abomination to the LORD," and in Rom. 14[:23]: "Whatever does not proceed from faith is sin."

But let us bring this first part to an end, though I am ready to go on with the argument if an opponent should arise. From all that has been said we conclude that the Mass was provided only for those who have a sad, afflicted, disturbed, perplexed, and erring conscience, and that they alone commune worthily. For, since the word of divine promise in this sacrament sets forth the forgiveness of sins, let all draw near fearlessly, whoever they may be, who are troubled by their sins, whether by remorse or by temptation. For this testament of Christ is the one remedy against sins, past, present, and future, if you but cling to it with unwavering faith and believe that what the words of the testament declare is freely granted to you. But if you do not believe this, you will never, anywhere, by any works or efforts of your own, be able to find peace of conscience. For faith alone means peace of conscience, while unbelief means only distress of conscience.

The Sacrament of Baptism

Blessed be God and the Father of our Lord Jesus Christ, who according to the riches of his mercy [Eph. 1:3, 7] has preserved in his church this sacrament at least, untouched and untainted by human ordinances, and has made it free to all nations and classes of people, and has not permitted it to be oppressed by the filth and great impiety of greed and superstitions. For he desired

141. The distinction of God's "alien" and "proper" work (*opus alienum—opus proprium*), derived from Isa. 28:21 ("For the LORD will rise up . . . to work his work—alien is his work"), can be found already in Luther's sermons in 1516 (e.g., WA 1:111–14). There he can speak of God's work as double (*duplex*) so that the gospel according to its proper function and intention is forgiveness and grace. Yet unbelief necessarily places one under its judgment, so that the gospel effects the opposite of its intended purpose, i.e., an alien work. Later Luther finds it clearer to correlate the language of alien and proper work with the distinction of law and gospel.

142. Gregory the Great, *Regula pastoralis* 1, 10: "For we all know well that, when one who is in disfavor is sent to intercede with an incensed person, the mind of the latter is provoked to greater severity." Cf. Gabriel Biel, *Canonis misse expositio*, lect. 27 C.

143. Gen. 4:5: "but for Cain and his offering he had no regard. So Cain was very angry, and his countenance fell."

Infant baptism as depicted
in *Catechismus* by Johannes Brenz
(1499–1570).

144. I.e., letters of indulgence.

145. Jerome's quote, from *Ep.* 130, 9, "Let us know nothing of penitence, lest the thought of it lead us into sin. It is a plank for those who have had the misfortune to be shipwrecked," echoes the earlier saying of Tertullian (c. 155–240) in his treatise *De poenitentia*: "That repentance, O sinner, like myself . . . do you so hasten to, so embrace, as a shipwrecked man the protection of some plank. This will draw you forth when sunk in the waves of sins, and will bear you forward into the port of the divine clemency." See also Lombard, *Sentences* 4, d. 14, c. 1: "As Jerome says, it is 'the second plank after shipwreck,' because, if anyone has corrupted by sin the clothing of innocence which he received at baptism, he may repair it by the remedy of penance. . . . Those who have fallen after baptism can

that by it little children, who were incapable of greed and superstition, might be initiated and sanctified in the simple faith of his Word; even today baptism has its chief blessing for them. But if the intention had been to give this sacrament to adults and older people, I do not believe that it could possibly have retained its power and its glory against the tyranny of greed and superstition which has overthrown all things divine among us. Here too the wisdom of the flesh would doubtless have devised its preparations and dignities, its reservations, restrictions, and other like snares for catching money, until water brought as high a price as parchment[144] does now.

But Satan, though he could not quench the power of baptism in little children, nevertheless succeeded in quenching it in all adults, so that now there are scarcely any who call to mind their own baptism, and still fewer who glory in it; so many other ways have been discovered for remitting sins and getting to heaven. The source of these false opinions is that dangerous saying of St. Jerome—either unhappily phrased or wrongly interpreted—in which he terms penance "the second plank after shipwreck," as if baptism were not penance.[145] Hence, when people have fallen into sin, they despair of the "first plank," which is the ship, as if it had gone under, and begin to put all their trust and faith in the second plank, which is penance.[146] This has given rise to those endless burdens of vows, religious orders, works, satisfactions, pilgrimages, indulgences, and monastic sects,[147] and from them in turn has arisen that flood of books, questions, opinions, and man-made ordinances which the whole world cannot contain. Thus the church of God is incomparably worse off under this tyranny than the synagogue or any other nation under heaven ever was.

It was the duty of the pontiffs to remove all these evils and to put forth every effort to recall Christians to the purity of baptism, so that they might understand what it means to be Christians and what Christians ought to do. But instead of this, their only work today is to lead the people as far astray as possible from their baptism, to immerse all people in the flood of their tyranny, and to cause the people of Christ (as the prophet says) to forget him days without number.[148] How unregenerate are all who bear the name of pontiff today! For they neither know nor do what is becoming to pontiffs, but they are ignorant of what they ought to know and do. They fulfill what Isa. 56[:10, 11] says:

"His watchmen are blind, they are all without knowledge; the shepherds also have no understanding; they have all turned to their own way, each to his own gain, etc."

[The First Part of Baptism: The Divine Promise]

Now, the first thing to be considered about baptism is the divine promise, which says: "The one who believes and is baptized will be saved" [Mark 16:16]. This promise must be set far above all the glitter of works, vows, religious orders, and whatever else human beings have introduced, for on it all our salvation depends. But we must so consider it as to exercise our faith in it, and have no doubt whatever that, once we have been baptized, we are saved. For unless faith is present or is conferred in baptism, baptism will profit us nothing; indeed, it will become a hindrance to us, not only at the moment when it is received, but throughout the rest of our lives. That kind of unbelief accuses God's promise of being a lie, and this is the greatest of all sins.[j] If we set ourselves to this exercise of faith, we shall at once perceive how difficult it is to believe this promise of God. For our human weakness, conscious of its sins, finds nothing more difficult to believe than that it is saved or will be saved; and yet, unless it does believe this, it cannot be saved, because it does not believe the truth of God that promises salvation.

This message should have been impressed upon the people untiringly, and this promise should have been dinned into their ears without ceasing. Their baptism should have been called to their minds again and again, and their faith constantly awakened and nourished. For just as the truth of this divine promise, once pronounced over us, continues until death, so our faith in it ought never to cease, but to be nourished and strengthened until death by the continual remembrance of this promise made to us in baptism. Therefore, when we rise from our sins or repent, we are merely returning to the power and the faith of baptism from which we fell, and finding our way back to the promise then made to us, which we deserted when we sinned. For the truth of the promise once made remains steadfast, always ready to receive us back with open arms when we return. And this, if I mistake not, is what they mean when they say, though obscurely,

be renewed by penance, but not by baptism; it is lawful for someone to repent several times, but not to be baptized several times."

146. This notion of penance as an emergency rescue stems from questions regarding the possibility and consequences of postbaptismal sin. A rigorist position is demonstrable throughout the early church, possibly already reflected in Heb. 6:4f., but definitively set forth by the second-century Christian text, *Shepherd of Hermes*. The angel in the *Shepherd* admits that though one who is baptized should live a life of purity (Mandate IV, 1:8-9; 2:1; 3:1), God has mercifully introduced a single means of restoration. "'But I tell you,' said he, 'after that great and holy calling, if a man be tempted by the devil and sin, he has *one repentance*, but if he sin and repent repeatedly it is unprofitable for such a man, for scarcely shall he live'" (Mandate IV, 3:4-6). Incidentally, Luther's question over the apostolic authorship of Hebrews focuses especially on Heb. 6:4f.

147. The loss of baptism as the rhythm and shape of the daily Christian forgiveness has, according to Luther, left a vacuum that was then filled by every effort to bring security and satisfaction. This list represents many of the false *Geistlichkeiten* that Luther wished to abolish or reform, i.e., spiritual/devotional practices common throughout the Middle Ages to deal with postbaptismal sin.

148. Jer. 2:32: "Can a girl forget her ornaments, or a bride her attire? Yet my people have forgotten me, days without number."

---

j See n. 105, p. 46.

149. Lombard, *Sentences* 4, d. 2, c. 2: "Now let us examine the sacrament of baptism, which is the first among the sacraments of the new grace." Also Pope Eugene IV (1383–1447) issued a bull at the Council of Florence (1439), *Exultate Deo*: "Holy baptism, which is the gateway to the spiritual life, holds the first place among all the sacraments; through it we are made members of Christ and of the body of the Church." Cf. also Biel, *Sentences* 4, d. 2, q. 1, a. 1, n. 1 A: "just as faith is the first and foundation of the rest of the virtues, so baptism is the chief of sacraments and their doorway."

that baptism is the first sacrament and the foundation of all the others, without which none of the others can be received.[149]

It will therefore be no small gain to penitents to remember above all their baptism, and, confidently calling to mind the divine promise which they have forsaken, acknowledge that promise before their Lord, rejoicing that they are still within the fortress of salvation because they have been baptized, and abhorring their wicked ingratitude in falling away from its faith and truth. Their hearts will find wonderful comfort and will be encouraged to hope for mercy when they consider that the promise which God made to them, which cannot possibly lie, is still unbroken and unchanged, and indeed, cannot be changed by sins, as Paul says (2 Tim. 2[:13]): "If we are faithless, he remains faithful—for he cannot deny himself." This truth of God, I say, will sustain them, so that if all else should fail, this truth, if they believe in it, will not fail them. In it the penitents have a shield against all assaults of the scornful enemy, an answer to the sins that disturb their conscience, an antidote for the dread of death and judgment, and a comfort in every temptation—namely, this one truth—when they say: "God is faithful in his promises, and I received his sign in baptism. If God is for me, who is against me?"[k,l]

The children of Israel, whenever they turned to repentance, remembered above all their exodus from Egypt, and remembering turned back to God who had brought them out. Moses impressed this memory and this protection upon them many times, and David afterwards did the same.[m] How much more ought we to remember our exodus from Egypt, and by this remembrance turn back to him who led us through the washing of regeneration,[n] remembrance of which is commended to us for this very reason! This can be done most fittingly in the sacrament of bread and wine. Indeed, in former times these three sacraments—penance, baptism, and the bread—were all celebrated at the same service, and each one supplemented the other. We

---

k   Rom. 8:31.

l   The original text of this paragraph is singular.

m Cf. Deut. 5:15; 6:12, 21; 8:14; Pss. 78:12f.; 80:8; 106:7f.; Jer. 2:5f.; Dan. 9:15.

n   Titus 3:5.

also read of a certain holy virgin who in every time of temptation made baptism her sole defense, saying simply, "I am a Christian"; and immediately the enemy recognized the power of baptism and of her faith, which clung to the truth of a promising God, and fled from her.[150]

Thus you see how rich a Christian is, that is, one who has been baptized! Even if those who have been baptized would, they could not lose their salvation, however much they sinned, unless they refused to believe. For no sin can condemn them save unbelief alone.[o] All other sins, so long as the faith in God's promise made in baptism returns or remains, are immediately blotted out through that same faith, or rather through the truth of God, because he cannot deny himself if you confess him and faithfully cling to him in his promise. But as for contrition, confession of sins, and satisfaction,[151] along with all those carefully devised human exercises: if you rely on them and neglect this truth of God, they will suddenly fail you and leave you more wretched than before. For whatever is done without faith in God's truth is vanity of vanities and vexation of spirit.[p]

You will likewise see how perilous, indeed, how false it is to suppose that penance is "the second plank after shipwreck," and how pernicious an error it is to believe that the power of baptism is broken, and the ship dashed to pieces, because of sin.[q] The ship remains one, solid, and invincible; it will never be broken up into separate "planks." In it are carried all those who are brought to the harbor of salvation, for it is the truth of God giving us its promise in the sacraments. Of course, it often happens that many rashly leap overboard into the sea and perish; these are those who abandon faith in the promise and plunge into sin. But the ship itself remains intact and holds its course unimpaired. If anyone is able somehow by grace to return to the ship, it is not on any plank, but in the solid ship itself that that person is carried to life. Such a person is the one who returns through faith to the abiding and enduring promise of God. Therefore Peter, in 1 Pet. 1, rebukes those who sin, because they have forgotten that

150. St. Blandina was martyred in 177 CE in Lyon under the reign of Marcus Aurelius (121–180). The account of her death comes from a letter reproduced by Eusebius (c. 265–c. 340) in his *Church History*; see *Hist. Eccl.* 5, 1, 19.

151. On these three parts of sacramental penance see Lombard, *Sentences* 4, d. 16, c. 1: "In the performance of penance, three things are to be considered, namely compunction of heart, confession of the mouth, satisfaction in deed. . . . Just as we offend God in three ways, namely by heart, mouth, hand, so also let us make satisfaction in three ways."

o   The original text of this section is singular.

p   Eccles. 1:2f.

q   See n. 145, p. 60.

152. Probably a reference to 2 Pet. 1:5-9, "For this very reason, you must make every effort to support your faith with goodness, and goodness with knowledge, and knowledge with self-control, and self-control with endurance, and endurance with godliness, and godliness with mutual affection, and mutual affection with love. For if these things are yours and are increasing among you, they keep you from being ineffective and unfruitful in the knowledge of our Lord Jesus Christ. For anyone who lacks these things is short-sighted and blind, and is forgetful of the cleansing of past sins."

153. Aquinas, *STh* I-II, q. 112, a. 5: ". . . man cannot judge with certainty whether he has grace." However, see the posthumous supplement *STh* III Suppl., q. 10, a. 4. For a helpful discussion of the difference between Luther and Aquinas on the certainty of salvation, see Otto H. Pesch, "Existential and Sapiential Theology—the Theological Confrontation between Luther and Thomas Aquinas," in Jared Wicks, S.J., ed., *Catholic Scholars Dialogue with Luther* (Chicago: Loyola University Press, 1970), 61–81.

154. In the effort to confess the entirety of one's sins, the penitent must also divulge the circumstances, that is, the related conditions that accompany the action, so that the priest may determine the nature of the sin committed and degree of guilt. Circumstances may turn a venial sin into a mortal sin.

155. The early Scholastic use of the terms *matter* and *form* was more general than the technical use in Aristotle. The "matter" of the sacrament is the elements of the sign (e.g., baptism = water) and the "form" is the words used in its sacramental use (e.g., baptism =

they were cleansed from their old sins, and he clearly rebukes their wicked unbelief and their ingratitude for the baptism they had received.[152]

What is the good, then, of writing so much about baptism and yet not teaching this faith in the promise? All the sacraments were instituted to nourish faith. Yet these godless men pass over it so completely as even to assert that a Christian dare not be certain of the forgiveness of sins or the grace of the sacraments.[153] With such wicked teaching they delude the world, and not only take captive, but altogether destroy, the sacrament of baptism, in which the chief glory of our conscience consists. Meanwhile they madly rage against the miserable souls of human beings with their contritions, anxious confessions, circumstances,[154] satisfactions, works, and endless other such absurdities. Therefore read with great caution the "Master of the *Sentences*" in his fourth book;[r] better yet, despise him with all his commentators, who at their best write only of the "matter" and "form" of the sacraments;[155] that is, they treat of the dead and death-dealing letter[156] of the sacraments, but leave untouched the spirit, life, and use, that is, the truth of the divine promise and our faith.

Beware, therefore, that the external pomp of works and the deceits of man-made ordinances do not deceive you, lest you wrong the divine truth and your faith. If you would be saved, you must begin with the faith of the sacraments, without any works whatever. The works will follow faith, but do not think too lightly of faith, for it is the most excellent and difficult of all works. Through it alone you will be saved, even if you should be compelled to do without any other works. For faith is a work of God, not of man, as Paul teaches.[157] The other works he works

r   Peter Lombard. Book 4 of the *Sentences* is dedicated to questions "On the Doctrine of Signs" (*De Doctrina Signorum*), i.e., the sacraments; see n. 56, p. 30 and n. 149, p. 62.

through us and with our help, but this one alone he works in us and without our help.

From this we can clearly see that in baptizing there is a difference between the human minister and God the author. For the man baptizes, and yet does not baptize. He baptizes in that he performs the work of immersing the person to be baptized; he does not baptize, because in so doing he acts not on his own authority but in God's stead. Hence we ought to receive baptism at human hands just as if Christ himself, indeed, God himself, were baptizing us with his own hands. For it is not man's baptism, but Christ's and God's baptism, which we receive by the hand of a man, just as everything else that we have through the hand of somebody else is God's alone. Therefore beware of making any distinction in baptism by ascribing the outward part to man and the inward part to God. Ascribe both to God alone, and look upon the person administering it as simply the vicarious instrument of God, by which the Lord sitting in heaven thrusts you under the water with his own hands, and promises you forgiveness of your sins, speaking to you upon earth with a human voice by the mouth of his minister.

This the words themselves indicate, when the minister says: "I baptize you in the name of the Father, and of the Son, and of the Holy Ghost. Amen," and not: "I baptize you in my own name." It is as though he said: "What I do, I do not by my own authority, but in the name and stead of God, so that you should regard it just as if our Lord himself had done it in a visible manner. The doer and the minister are different persons, but the work of both is the same work, or rather, it is the work of the doer alone, through my ministry." For I hold that "in the name of"[158] refers to the person of the doer, so that the name of the Lord is not only to be uttered and invoked while the work is being done; but the work itself is to be done as something not one's own—in the name and stead of another. In this sense Christ says in Matt. 24[:5], "Many will come in my name," and Rom. 1[:5] says, "Through whom we have received grace and apostleship to bring about obedience for his name among all the nations."

This view I heartily endorse, for there is great comfort and a mighty aid to faith in the knowledge that one has been baptized, not by man, but by the Triune God himself, through a man acting among us in his name. This will put an end to that idle dispute about the "form" of baptism, as they term the words which

"I baptize you in the name . . . ," etc.). See, for example, Lombard, *Sentences* 4, d. 3, c. 2: "On the Form of Baptism: But what is that word, at whose addition to the element the sacrament is brought about?—Truth teaches it to you, who, laying down the form of this sacrament, said to the disciples: 'Go, teach all nations, baptizing them in the name . . .'"; Thomas Aquinas, adopted the earlier terminology but began interpreting it in a more precise Aristotelian manner, e.g., *STh* III, q. 60, a. 7: "As stated above, in the sacraments the words are as the form, and sensible things are as the matter. Now in all things composed of matter and form, the determining principle is on the part of the form, which is as it were the end and terminus of the matter. Consequently, for the being of a thing the need of a determinate form is prior to the need of determinate matter: for determinate matter is needed that it may be adapted to the determinate form. Since, therefore, in the sacraments determinate sensible things are required, which are as the sacramental matter, much more is there need in them of a determinate form of words."

156. 2 Cor. 3:6: "for the letter kills, but the Spirit gives life." Luther can use the language of this text to indicate the external and superficial versus the inner and essential, or he can use it in the Augustinian sense of the law versus grace.

157. Eph. 2:8: "For by grace you have been saved through faith, and this is not your own doing; it is the gift of God."

158. The Latin *in nomine* can certainly have the meaning "by the authority of"; however, the Greek of Matthew 28 from which the baptismal formula is

159. See the bull *Exultate Deo* (1439), from the Council of Florence: "The form is: 'I baptize you in the name of the Father and of the Son and of the Holy Spirit.' But we do not deny that true baptism is conferred by the following words: 'May this servant of Christ be baptized in the name of the Father and of the Son and of the Holy Spirit'; or, 'This person is baptized by my hands in the name of the Father and of the Son and of the Holy Spirit.' Since the Holy Trinity is the principle cause from which baptism has its power and the minister is the instrumental cause who exteriorly bestows the sacrament, the sacrament is conferred if the action is performed by the minister with the invocation of the Holy Trinity."

160. Alexander of Hales (1185–1245) denied the validity of a baptism performed "in the name of Jesus"; however, see Lombard, *Sentences* 4, d. 3, c. 3: "the apostles baptized in the name of Christ. But in this name [i.e., of Christ], as Ambrose explains, the whole Trinity is understood."

161. St. Genesius was a popular legendary saint, supposedly martyred under Emperor Diocletian (245–311). According to the legend, Genesius received a mock baptism on stage in ridicule of Christianity, but the effect was his sudden conversion.

162. Representatives of this view include Hugh of St. Victor (c. 1096–1141), *On the Sacraments of the Christian Faith* 1, 1, 1: "a sacrament, through its being sanctified, contains an invisible grace"; and Aquinas, *STh* III, q. 62, a. 4: "there

derived—*eis to onoma*—may also have the sense of "into the name." In this case, the meaning would be similar to Rom. 6:3, "baptized into Christ . . . into his death."

are used. The Greeks say: "May the servant of Christ be baptized," while the Latins say: "I baptize."[159] Others again, adhering rigidly to their pedantry, condemn the use of the words, "I baptize you in the name of Jesus Christ,"[160] although it is certain the apostles used this formula in baptizing, as we read in the Acts of the Apostles;[s] they would allow no other form to be valid than this: "I baptize you in the name of the Father, and of the Son, and of the Holy Ghost. Amen." But their contention is in vain, for they bring no proof, but merely assert their own dreams. Baptism truly saves in whatever way it is administered, if only it is administered not in the name of man, but in the name of the Lord. Indeed, I have no doubt that if anyone receives baptism in the name of the Lord, even if the wicked minister should not give it in the name of the Lord, he would yet be truly baptized in the name of the Lord. For the power of baptism depends not so much on the faith or use of the one who confers it as on the faith or use of the one who receives it. We have an example of this in the story of a certain actor who was baptized in jest.[161] These and similar perplexing disputes and questions are raised for us by those who ascribe nothing to faith and everything to works and rituals, whereas we owe everything to faith alone and nothing to rituals. Faith makes us free in spirit from all those doubts and mere opinions.

[The Second Part of Baptism: The Sign]

The second part of baptism is the sign, or sacrament, which is that immersion in water from which it derives its name, for the Greek *baptizō* means "I immerse," and *baptisma* means "immersion." For, as has been said, along with the divine promises signs have also been given to picture that which the words signify, or as they now say, that which the sacrament "effectively signifies." We shall see how much truth there is in this.

A great majority have supposed that there is some hidden spiritual power in the word and water, which works the grace of God in the soul of the recipient.[162] Others deny this and hold that there is no power in the sacraments, but that grace is given by God alone, who according to his covenant is present in the

---

s   E.g., Acts 2:38; 8:16; 10:48; 19:5.

sacraments which he has instituted.[163] Yet all are agreed that the sacraments are "effective signs" of grace, and they reach this conclusion by this one argument: if the sacraments of the New Law were mere signs, there would be no apparent reason why they should surpass those of the Old Law.[164] Hence they have been driven to attribute such great powers to the sacraments of the New Law that they think the sacraments benefit even those who are in mortal sin; neither faith nor grace are required—it is sufficient that no obstacle be set in the way, that is, no actual intention to sin again.[165]

Such views, however, must be carefully avoided and shunned, because they are godless and infidel, contrary to faith and inconsistent with the nature of the sacraments. For it is an error to hold that the sacraments of the New Law differ from those of the Old Law in the effectiveness of their signs. For in this respect they are the same. The same God who now saves us by baptism and the bread saved Abel by his sacrifice,[t] Noah by the rainbow,[u] Abraham by circumcision,[v] and all the others by their respective signs. So far as the signs are concerned, there is no difference between a sacrament of the Old Law and one of the New, provided that by the Old Law you mean that which God did among the patriarchs and other fathers in the days of the Law. But those signs which were given to the patriarchs and fathers must be clearly distinguished from the legal symbols which Moses instituted in his law, such as the priestly usages concerning vestments, vessels, foods, houses, and the like. For these are vastly different, not only from the sacraments of the New Law, but also from those signs which God occasionally gave to the fathers living under the law, such as the sign of Gideon's fleece,[w] Manoah's sacrifice,[x] or that which Isaiah offered to Ahaz in Isa. 7.[y] In each of these alike some promise was given which required faith in God.

t   Gen. 4:4.
u   Gen. 6:13-22.
v   Gen. 17:10f.
w   Judg. 6:36-40.
x   Judg. 13:16-23.
y   Isa. 7:10-16.

is nothing to hinder an instrumental spiritual power from being in a body; in so far as a body can be moved by a particular spiritual substance so as to produce a particular spiritual effect . . . it is in this way that a spiritual power is in the sacraments, inasmuch as they are ordained by God unto the production of a spiritual effect."

163. Aquinas, though in disagreement, correctly describes this alternate position held by theologians such as Bonaventure (1221–1274) and Duns Scotus (c. 1266–1308), in *STh* III, q. 62, a. 4: "Those who hold that the sacraments do not cause grace save by a certain coincidence, deny the sacraments any power that is itself productive of the sacramental effect, and hold that the Divine power assists the sacraments and produces their effect." See also Gabriel Biel, *Sentences* 4, d. 1, q. 1, a. 1, c. 1, in which the sacraments are not effective intrinsically (*ex natura rei*) but because of the will and covenant of God (*ex voluntate Dei*).

164. Cf. Lombard, *Sentences* 4, d. 1, 3: "Observances of the Old Law are better called signs than sacraments. For those things which were instituted only for the sake of signifying are merely signs, and not sacraments; such were the carnal sacrifices and the ceremonial observances of the Old Law, which could never justify those who offered them." Aquinas, *STh* III, q. 62, a. 6: "it is therefore clear that the sacraments of the New Law do reasonably derive the power of justification from Christ's Passion, which is the cause of man's righteousness; whereas the sacraments of the Old Law did not."

165. The Scholastic doctrine that the sacraments of the New Testament intrinsically confer grace (*ex opere operato*) was conditioned by the absence of any spiritual obstacle. For example, if one receives the sacrament under false pretenses, the substance of the sacrament would still be received but the grace would not benefit the recipient (cf. Lombard, *Sentences* 4, d. 4, c. 2; Aquinas, *STh* III, q. 69, a. 9). Gabriel Biel identifies a mortal sin as an obstacle, *Sentences* 4, d. 1, q. 3, n. 2 B: "unless one impedes by an obstacle of mortal sin, grace is conferred."

The difference, then, between the legal symbols and the new and old signs is that the legal symbols do not have attached to them any word of promise requiring faith. Hence they are not signs of justification, for they are not sacraments of the faith that alone justifies, but only sacraments of works. Their whole power and nature consisted in works, not in faith. Those who performed them fulfilled them, even if they did it without faith. But our signs or sacraments, as well as those of the fathers, have attached to them a word of promise which requires faith, and they cannot be fulfilled by any other work. Hence they are signs or sacraments of justification, for they are sacraments of justifying faith and not of works. Their whole efficacy, therefore, consists in faith itself, not in the doing of a work. Those who believe them, fulfill them, even if they should not do a single work. This is the origin of the saying: "Not the sacrament, but the faith of the sacrament, justifies." Thus circumcision did not justify Abraham and his seed, and yet the Apostle calls it the seal of the righteousness by faith,[z] because faith in the promise, to which circumcision was added, justified him and fulfilled what the circumcision signified. For faith was the spiritual circumcision of the foreskin of the heart,[a] which was symbolized by the literal circumcision of the flesh. In the same way it was obviously not Abel's sacrifice that justified him, but it was his faith[b] by which he offered himself wholly to God, and this was symbolized by the outward sacrifice.

Thus it is not baptism that justifies or benefits anyone, but it is faith in that word of promise to which baptism is added. This faith justifies, and fulfills that which baptism signifies. For faith is the submersion of the old person and the emerging of the new.[c] Therefore the new sacraments cannot differ from the old sacraments, for both alike have the divine promises and the same spirit of faith, although they do differ vastly from the old symbols—on account of the word of promise, which is the sole effective means of distinguishing them. Even so, today, the outward show of vestments, holy places, foods, and all the endless

z   Rom. 4:11.

a   Deut. 10:16; Jer. 4:4.

b   Heb. 11:4.

c   Cf. Eph. 4:22-24; Col. 3:9-10.

ceremonies doubtless symbolize excellent things to be fulfilled in the spirit, yet, because there is no word of divine promise attached to these things, they can in no way be compared with the signs of baptism and the bread. Neither do they justify, nor benefit one in any way, since they are fulfilled in their very observance, even in their observance apart from faith. For while they are taking place, or being performed, they are being fulfilled, as the Apostle says of them in Col. 2[:22]: "Which all perish as they are used, according to human precepts and doctrines." The sacraments, on the contrary, are not fulfilled when they are taking place, but when they are being believed.

It cannot be true, therefore, that there is contained in the sacraments a power efficacious for justification, or that they are "effective signs" of grace. All such things are said to the detriment of faith, and out of ignorance of the divine promise. Unless you should call them "effective" in the sense that they certainly and effectively impart grace where faith is unmistakably present. But it is not in this sense that efficacy is now ascribed to them; as witness the fact that they are said to benefit all people, even the wicked and unbelieving, provided they do not set an obstacle in the way [d] —as if such unbelief were not in itself the most obstinate and hostile of all obstacles to grace. To such an extent have they exerted themselves to turn the sacrament into a command and faith into a work. For if the sacrament confers grace on me because I receive it, then indeed I receive grace by virtue of my work, and not by faith; and I gain not the promise in the sacrament but only the sign instituted and commanded by God. Thus you see clearly how completely the sacraments have been misunderstood by the theologians of the *Sentences*.[e] In their discussions of the sacraments they have taken no account either of faith or of promise. They cling only to the sign and the use of the sign, and draw us away from faith to the work, away from the word to the sign. Thus, as I have said, they have not only taken the sacraments captive, but have completely destroyed them, as far as they were able.

d   See n. 165, pp. 67–68.
e   See n. 56, p. 30.

Therefore let us open our eyes and learn to pay heed more to the word than to the sign, more to faith than to the work or use of the sign. We know that wherever there is a divine promise, there faith is required, and that these two are so necessary to each other that neither can be effective apart from the other. For it is not possible to believe unless there is a promise, and the promise is not established unless it is believed. But where these two meet, they give a real and most certain efficacy to the sacraments. Hence, to seek the efficacy of the sacrament apart from the promise and apart from the faith is to labor in vain and to find condemnation. Thus Christ says: "The one who believes and is baptized will be saved; but the one who does not believe will be condemned" [Mark 16:16]. He shows us in this word that faith is such a necessary part of the sacrament that it can save even without the sacrament, and for this reason he did not add: "The one who does not believe, and is not baptized."

[Baptism Signifies Death and Resurrection]

Baptism, then, signifies two things—death and resurrection,[f] that is, full and complete justification. When the minister immerses the child in the water it signifies death, and when he draws it forth again it signifies life. Thus Paul expounds it in Rom. 6[:4]: "Therefore we have been buried with [Christ] by baptism into death, so that just as Christ was raised from the dead by the glory of the Father, so we too might walk in newness of life." This death and resurrection we call the new creation, regeneration, and spiritual birth.[g] This should not be understood only allegorically as the death of sin and the life of grace, as many understand it, but as actual death and resurrection. For baptism is not a false sign. Neither does sin completely die, nor grace completely rise, until the sinful body that we carry about in this life is destroyed, as the Apostle says in the same passage.[166] For as long as we are in the flesh, the desires of the flesh stir and are stirred. For this reason, as soon as we begin to believe, we also begin to die to this world and live to God in the life to come; so

166. Rom. 6:6-7: "We know that our old self was crucified with him so that the body of sin might be destroyed, and we might no longer be enslaved to sin. For whoever has died is freed from sin."

f   Cf. *The Holy Sacrament of Baptism* (1519), LW 35:30f.
g   Cf. 2 Cor. 5:17; Titus 3:5; John 3:6.

that faith is truly a death and a resurrection, that is, it is that spiritual baptism into which we are submerged and from which we rise.

It is therefore indeed correct to say that baptism is a washing away of sins, but the expression is too mild and weak to bring out the full significance of baptism, which is rather a symbol of death and resurrection. For this reason, I would have those who are to be baptized completely immersed in the water, as the word says and as the mystery indicates.[h] Not because I deem this necessary, but because it would be well to give to a thing so perfect and complete a sign that is also complete and perfect. And this is doubtless the way in which it was instituted by Christ. The sinner does not so much need to be washed as he needs to die, in order to be wholly renewed and made another creature, and to be conformed to the death and resurrection of Christ, with whom he dies and rises again through baptism.[i] Although you may say that when Christ died and rose again he was washed clean of mortality, that is a less forceful way of putting it than if you said that he was completely changed and renewed. Similarly it is far more forceful to say that baptism signifies that we die in every way and rise to eternal life, than to say that it signifies merely that we are washed clean of sins.

Here again you see that the sacrament of baptism, even with respect to its sign, is not a matter of the moment, but something permanent. Although the ceremony itself is soon over the thing it signifies continues until we die, yes, even until we rise on the last day. For as long as we live we are continually doing that which baptism signifies, that is, we die and rise again. We die, not only mentally and spiritually by renouncing the sins and vanities of this world, but in very truth we begin to leave this bodily life and to lay hold on the life to come, so that there is, as they say, a "real" and bodily passing out of this world unto the Father.

We must therefore beware of those who have reduced the power of baptism to such small and slender dimensions that, while they say that by it grace is indeed poured in, they maintain that afterwards it is poured out again through sin, and

h   Cf. *The Holy Sacrament of Baptism* (1519), LW 35:30f.
i   Cf. Rom. 6:8.

that then one must reach heaven by another way, as if baptism had now become entirely useless.[j] Do not hold such a view, but understand that this is the significance of baptism, that through it you die and live again. Therefore, whether by penance or by any other way, you can only return to the power of your baptism, and do again that which you were baptized to do and which your baptism signified. Baptism never becomes useless, unless you despair and refuse to return to its salvation. You may indeed wander away from the sign for a time, but the sign is not therefore useless. Thus, you have been once baptized in the sacrament, but you need continually to be baptized by faith, continually to die and continually to live. Baptism swallowed up your whole body and gave it forth again; in the same way that which baptism signifies should swallow up your whole life, body and soul, and give it forth again at the last day, clad in the robe of glory and immortality. We are therefore never without the sign of baptism nor without the thing it signifies. Indeed, we need continually to be baptized more and more, until we fulfill the sign perfectly at the last day.

You will understand, therefore, that whatever we do in this life which mortifies the flesh or quickens the spirit has to do with our baptism. The sooner we depart this life, the more speedily we fulfill our baptism;[k] and the more cruelly we suffer, the more successfully do we conform to our baptism. Hence the church was at its best at the time when martyrs were being put to death every day and accounted as sheep for the slaughter,[l] for then the power of baptism reigned supreme in the church, whereas today we have lost sight of this power amid the multitude of human works and doctrines. For our whole life should be baptism, and the fulfilling of the sign or sacrament of baptism, since we have been set free from all else and given over to baptism alone, that is, to death and resurrection.

This glorious liberty of ours and this understanding of baptism have been taken captive in our day, and to whom can we give the blame except the Roman pontiff with his despotism? More than all others, as chief shepherd it was his first duty to proclaim this doctrine and defend this liberty, as Paul says in 1 Cor. 4[:1]:

---

j   See n. 146, p. 61.

k   Cf. *The Holy Sacrament of Baptism* (1519), LW 35:30f.

l   Ps. 44:22; Rom. 8:36.

"This is how one should regard us, as servants of Christ and stewards of the mysteries, or sacraments, of God." Instead he seeks only to oppress us with his decrees and laws, and to ensnare us as captives to his tyrannical power. By what right, I ask you, does the pope impose his laws upon us (to say nothing of his wicked and damnable neglect to teach us these mysteries)? Who gave him power to deprive us of this liberty of ours, granted to us in baptism? One thing only, as I have said, has been enjoined upon us to do all the days of our lives—to be baptized, that is, to be put to death and to live again through faith in Christ. This and this alone should have been taught, especially by the chief shepherd. But now faith is passed over in silence, and the church is smothered with endless laws concerning works and ceremonies; the power and understanding of baptism are set aside, and faith in Christ is obstructed.

Therefore I say: Neither pope nor bishop nor any other person has the right to impose a single syllable of law upon Christians without their[m] consent; if anyone does, it is done in the spirit of tyranny. Therefore the prayers, fasts, donations, and whatever else the pope ordains and demands in all of his decrees, as numerous as they are iniquitous, he demands and ordains without any right whatever; and he sins against the liberty of the church whenever he attempts any such thing. Hence it has come to pass that the churchmen of our day are such vigorous guardians of "ecclesiastical liberty"—that is, of wood and stone, of lands and rents[167] (for to such an extent has "ecclesiastical" today come to mean the same as "spiritual"!). Yet with such verbal fictions they not only take captive the true liberty of the church; they utterly destroy it, even worse than the Turk, and in opposition to the word of the Apostle: "Do not become slaves of men" [1 Cor. 7:23]. For to be subjected to their statutes and tyrannical laws is indeed to become slaves of men.

This impious and desperate tyranny is fostered by the pope's disciples, who here twist and pervert that saying of Christ: "He who hears you hears me" [Luke 10:16]. With puffed cheeks they inflate this saying to a great size in support of their own ordinances. Though Christ spoke this word to the apostles when they

167. The word *liberty* (Lat. *libertas*) gained a new meaning and usage in the Middle Ages, especially in the context of feudal society. Whereas Christian liberty was expressed as freedom from the bondage of sin and death in order to be a servant of Christ (e.g., Rom. 6.6f.; Gal. 5:1; 1 Cor. 7:22f.), liberty in the feudal system indicated one's possession of power and jurisdiction— usually over property—without external coercion or limits. Thus, granting a liberty was to grant a privilege. Clergy already began receiving such liberties in the age of Constantine, but as the church participated in the emerging feudal system as a landowner, the notion of "ecclesiastical liberty" had more to do with political and economic jurisdiction than liberty in a spiritual or theological sense. Luther is exploiting this irony in his comments here. Luther would set forth a very different sense of "freedom" in his subsequent treatise, *The Freedom of the Christian* (1520). For more on "liberty" in the Middle Ages and its impact on the church, see Gerd Tellenbach, *Church, State and Christian Society at the Time of the Investiture Controversy* (Oxford: Oxford University Press, 1938).

m Singular in the original.

went forth to preach the gospel, and though it should apply only to the gospel, they pass over the gospel and apply it only to their fables. For he says in John 10[:27, 5]: "My sheep hear my voice, but the voice of a stranger they do not hear." He left us the gospel so that the pontiffs might sound the voice of Christ. Instead they sound their own voices, and yet hope to be heard. Moreover, the Apostle says that he was not sent to baptize, but to preach the gospel." Therefore, no one is obliged to obey the ordinances of the pope, or required to listen to him, except when he teaches the gospel and Christ. And the pope should teach nothing but faith without any restrictions. But since Christ says, "He who hears you [plural] hears me" [Luke 10:16], why does not the pope also hear others? Christ does not say to Peter alone, "He who hears you" [singular]. In short, where there is true faith, there the word of faith must of necessity be also. Why then does not an unbelieving pope now and then hear a believing servant of his, who has the word of faith? Blindness, sheer blindness, reigns among the pontiffs.

Others, even more shameless, arrogantly ascribe to the pope the power to make laws, on the basis of Matt. 16[:19], "Whatever you bind, etc.," although Christ in this passage treats of binding and loosing sins, not of taking the whole church captive and oppressing it with laws. So this tyranny treats everything with its own lying words and violently twists and perverts the words of God. I admit indeed that Christians ought to bear this accursed tyranny just as they would bear any other violence of this world, according to Christ's word: "If any one strikes you on the right cheek, turn to him the other also" [Matt. 5:39]. But this is my complaint: that the godless pontiffs boastfully claim to do this by right, that they pretend to be seeking the church's welfare with this Babylon of theirs, and that they foist this fiction upon all people. For if they did these things and we suffered their violence, both sides being well aware that it was godlessness and tyranny, then we might easily number it among those things that contribute to the mortifying of this life and the fulfilling of our baptism, and might with a good conscience glory in the inflicted injury. But now they seek to deprive us of this consciousness of

---

n   1 Cor. 1:17.

our liberty, and would have us believe that what they do is well done, and must not be censured or complained of as wrongdoing. Being wolves, they masquerade as shepherds, and being Antichrists, they wish to be honored as Christ.

I lift my voice simply on behalf of liberty and conscience, and I confidently cry: No law, whether of men or of angels, may rightfully be imposed upon Christians without their consent, for we are free of all laws. And if any laws are imposed upon us, we must bear them in such a way as to preserve that sense of freedom which knows and affirms with certainty that an injustice is being done to it, even though it glories in bearing this injustice—so taking care neither to justify the tyrant nor to murmur against his tyranny. "Now who is there to harm you," says Peter, "if you are zealous for what is right?" [1 Pet. 3:13]. "All things work together for good to them that are the elect" [Rom. 8:28].

Nevertheless, since but few know this glory of baptism and the blessedness of Christian liberty, and cannot know them because of the tyranny of the pope, I for one will disengage myself, and keep my conscience free by bringing this charge against the pope and all his papists: Unless they will abolish their laws and ordinances, and restore to Christ's churches their liberty and have it taught among them, they are guilty of all the souls that perish under this miserable captivity, and the papacy is truly the kingdom of Babylon and of the very Antichrist.[168] For who is "the man of sin" and "the son of perdition" [2 Thess. 2:3] but he who with his doctrines and his laws increases the sins and perdition of souls in the church, while sitting in the church as if he were God?[169] All this the papal tyranny has fulfilled, and more than fulfilled, these many centuries. It has extinguished faith, obscured the sacraments and oppressed the gospel; but its own laws, which are not only impious and sacrilegious, but even barbarous and foolish, it has decreed and multiplied without end.

Behold, then, our miserable captivity. "How lonely sits the city that was full of people! How like a widow has she become, she that was great among the nations! She that was a princess among the cities has become a vassal. She has none to comfort her; all her friends have dealt treacherously with her, etc." [Lam. 1:1-2]. There are so many ordinances, so many rites, so many sects,[170] so many vows, so many exertions, and so many works in which Christians are engaged today, that they lose sight of their baptism. Because of this swarm of locusts, palmerworms, and

168. Calling the pope the Antichrist was not uncommon rhetoric, especially since the Western Schism (1378-1417). However, Luther's designation is more than rhetoric. He first privately floated the idea in a letter to a friend, Wenceslas Link (1482-1547), after his encounter with the papal legate, Cardinal Cajetan, in 1518, WA Br 1:270. With the threat of excommunication and no indication that the papacy would change its course, Luther finally put the epithet in print in his 1520 treatise against Augustinus von Alveld (see n.14, p. 15), *On the Papacy in Rome, Against the Most Celebrated Romanist in Leipzig,* LW 39:49-104. For a helpful overview on the question, see Robert Rosin, "The Papacy in Perspective: Luther's Reform and Rome," in *Concordia Journal* 29 (October 2003): 407-26.

169. 2 Thess. 2:3-4: "Let no one deceive you in any way; for that day will not come unless the rebellion comes first and the lawless one is revealed, the one destined for destruction. He opposes and exalts himself above every so-called god or object of worship, so that he takes his seat in the temple of God, declaring himself to be God."

170. "Sects" here is taken to mean the various rival monastic orders and divisions within Scholastic theology.

171. Cf. Augustine, *Against Two Letters of the Pelagians*, I, 40: "in the Church of the Savior, infants believe by means of other people, even as they have derived those sins which are remitted them in baptism from other people"; Lombard, *Sentences* 4, d. 4, c. 2: "remission is not given in baptism to children without someone else's faith, since they are unable to have their own"; Aquinas, *STh* III, d. 68, a. 9: "Just as a child, when he is being baptized, believes not by himself but by others, so is he examined not by himself but through others, and these in answer confess the Church's faith in the child's stead, who is aggregated to this faith by the sacrament of faith."

172. Luther's point is somewhat different from the traditional understanding of the *fides aliena*, i.e., grace given through the faith of another. The faith of the church or of the sponsors does not stand in as proxy for the child's faith; rather, it is faith that acts in prayer and thus intercedes on behalf of the child. As an answer to this prayer, God grants the child the personal faith necessary to receive baptism. Luther would make the same point later when advising one on how to comfort a mother of a stillborn or miscarriage: "God accomplishes much through the faith and longing of another, even a stranger, even though there is still no personal faith. But this is given through the channel of another's intercession, as in the Gospel Christ raised the widow's son at Nain because of the prayers of his mother apart from the faith of the son" (LW 43:250).

Luther's use of the term *fides infusa* ("the pouring in of faith") is also different from the Scholastic usage which, following Aristotelian ethics, approximates the gift of the theological virtues (faith, hope, and love) to the

cankerworms,[o] no one is able to remember that he is baptized, or what blessings baptism has brought him. We should be even as little children, when they are newly baptized, who engage in no efforts or works, but are free in every way, secure and saved solely through the glory of their baptism. For we are indeed little children, continually baptized anew in Christ.

In contradiction to what has been said, some might cite the baptism of infants who do not comprehend the promise of God and cannot have the faith of baptism; so that therefore either faith is not necessary or else infant baptism is without effect. Here I say what all say: Infants are aided by the faith of others, namely, those who bring them for baptism.[171] For the Word of God is powerful enough, when uttered, to change even a godless heart, which is no less unresponsive and helpless than any infant. So through the prayer of the believing church which presents it, a prayer to which all things are possible,[p] the infant is changed, cleansed, and renewed by the pouring in of faith [*fide infusa*].[172] Nor should I doubt that even a godless adult could be changed, in any of the sacraments, if the same church prayed for and presented him, as we read of the paralytic in the Gospel, who was healed through the faith of others.[q] I should be ready to admit that in this sense the sacraments of the New Law are efficacious in conferring grace, not only to those who do not,

o   Cf. Joel 1:4.

p   Cf. Mark 9:23.

q   Cf. Mark 2:3-12.

but even to those who do most obstinately present an obstacle.[173] What obstacle cannot be removed by the faith of the church and the prayer of faith? Do we not believe that Stephen converted Paul the Apostle by this power?[174] But then the sacraments do what they do not by their own power, but by the power of faith, without which they do nothing at all, as I have said.

The question remains whether an unborn infant, with only a hand or a foot projecting from the womb, can be baptized. Here I will confess my ignorance and make no hasty decision. I am not sure whether the reason they give is sufficient—that in any part of the body whatsoever the entire soul resides. For it is not the soul but the body that is externally baptized with water. But neither do I share the view of those who insist that he who is not yet born cannot be born again (even though it has considerable force).[175] I leave these things to the teaching of the Spirit, and "meanwhile allow everyone to enjoy his own opinion" [Rom. 14:5].

[Religious Vows Versus Baptism]

One thing I will add—and I wish that I could persuade everyone to do it—namely, that all vows should be completely abolished and avoided, whether of religious orders, or about pilgrimages or about any works whatsoever, that we may remain in that which is

acquisition of other virtues, namely, through the acquiring of a habit (*habitus*). But Luther is only stressing that faith is a divine gift with this phrase. Luther's critical engagement with the Scholastic teaching occurs also in 1520: *Disputatio de fide infusa et acquisita*, WA 6:85f. See also Reinhard Schwarz, *Fides, spes und caritas beim jungen Luther: unter besonderer Berücksichtigung der mittelalterlichen Tradition* (Berlin: Walter de Gruyter, 1962). The question of the possibility of faith in an infant is taken up by Luther more thoroughly in his treatise *Concerning Rebaptism: A Letter to Two Pastors* (1528), LW 40:225–62.

173. For the notion of setting an "obstacle" against the reception of grace, see n. 165, pp. 67–68.

174. Acts 7:58—8:1: "Then they dragged him out of the city and began to stone him; and the witnesses laid their coats at the feet of a young man named Saul. While they were stoning Stephen, he prayed, 'Lord Jesus, receive my spirit.' Then he knelt down and cried out in a loud voice, 'Lord, do not hold this sin against them.' When he had said this, he died. And Saul approved of their killing him." Augustine makes this point in a sermon on the birthday of St. Stephen, *Sermo* 382, 4, 4: "For if the martyr Stephen did not pray as he did, the church would not have Paul today."

175. Augustine held this opinion; cf. *Ep.* 187, 9: "No one can be reborn before being born." This opinion was carried on into much of the Scholastic tradition, for example, Lombard, *Sentences* 4, d. 6, c. 3. Aquinas holds an interesting middle position, *STh* III, q. 68, a. 11: "If, however, the head, wherein the senses are rooted, appear first, it should be baptized, in cases of danger: nor should it be baptized again, if perfect birth should ensue. And seemingly the same should be done in cases of danger no matter what part of the body appears first. But as none of the exterior parts of the body belong to its integrity in the same degree as the head, some hold that since the matter is doubtful, whenever any other part of the body has been baptized, the child, when perfect birth has taken place, should be baptized with the form: 'If you are not baptized, I baptize you,' etc."

176. Luther's concern is with the view that religious and monastic vows have set up a spiritual standard above and beyond the sacrament of baptism. In the late-medieval context, members of the monastic life and, by derivation, the clerical office, were regarded as belonging to a higher spiritual class than ordinary lay Christians. After martyrdom, monasticism was long regarded as the religious ideal of Christianity. In an attempt to embody the sacrificial, radical tenets in the Gospels, the monastic distinguished himself from the ordinary Christian by his vows of poverty, chastity, and obedience. The Ten Commandments were important, but "if you would be perfect," said the Lord, "sell all you have, give it to the poor, and come follow me." Pursuing the path the "perfect" those who took up monastic vows could even regard them as a kind of second baptism. But in Luther's earlier treatise, *The Address to the Christian Nobility* (1520), he argued that all ordinary Christians were truly spiritual and religious. Only faith made one spiritual, and the life of the laity was a true religious sacrifice and worship when lived out from that faith. Likewise the priesthood—it was not ordination but baptism that made one priests (1 Pet. 2:9). See TAL 1:382.

supremely religious and most rich in works—the freedom of baptism.[176] It is impossible to say how much that most widespread delusion of vows detracts from baptism and obscures the knowledge of Christian liberty, to say nothing now of the unspeakable and infinite peril of souls which that mania for making vows and that ill-advised rashness daily increase. O most godless pontiffs and unregenerate pastors, who slumber on unheeding and indulge in your evil lusts, without pity for this most dreadful and perilous "ruin of Joseph"! [Amos 6:4-6].

Vows should either be abolished by a general edict, especially those taken for life, and all people recalled to the vows of baptism, or else everyone should be diligently warned not to take a vow rashly. No one should be encouraged to do so; indeed, permission should be given only with difficulty and reluctance. For we have vowed enough in baptism, more than we can ever fulfill; if we give ourselves to the keeping of this one vow, we shall have all we can do. But now we traverse sea and land to make many proselytes;[r] we fill the world with priests, monks, and nuns, and imprison them all in lifelong vows. You will find those who argue and decree that a work done in fulfillment of a vow ranks higher than one done without a vow, and in heaven is to be rewarded above others with I know not what great rewards. Blind and godless Pharisees, who measure righteousness and holiness by the greatness, number, or other quality of the works! But God measures them by faith alone, and with him there is no difference among works, except insofar as there is a difference in faith.

With such bombast wicked men by their inventions puff up human opinion and human works, in order to lure on the unthinking Masses who are almost always led by the glitter of works to make shipwreck of their faith, to forget their baptism, and to injure their Christian liberty. For a vow is a kind of law or requirement. When vows are multiplied, laws and works are necessarily multiplied, and when these are multiplied, faith is extinguished and the liberty of baptism is taken captive. Others, not content with these wicked allurements, assert in addition that entrance into a religious order is like a new baptism, which may afterward be repeated as often as the purpose to live

r   Matt. 23:15.

the monastic life is renewed. Thus these votaries have appropriated to themselves all righteousness, salvation, and glory, and left to those who are merely baptized nothing to compare with them. Now the Roman pontiff, that fountain and source of all superstitions, confirms, approves, and adorns this mode of life with high-sounding bulls[177] and dispensations, while no one deems baptism worthy of even a thought. And with such glittering pomp, as I have said, they drive the pliable people of Christ into the "Clashing Rocks,"[178] so that in their ingratitude toward baptism they presume to achieve greater things by their works than others achieve by their faith.

177. A "bull" (*bulla*) is an official papal decree. The name is derived from the seal on the document that guaranteed its authenticity.

178. The Latin has *Symplegades*—the name of the rocks at the Bosphorus, the entrance to the Black Sea, which, according to the Greek myth of Jason and the Argonauts, would leave their moorings and crush all who attempted to pass through. The sense here is that monastic vows are put forth as a greater sense of security than mere faith, but like the Symplegades they are deceptively dangerous.

This fresco, painted by Fra Angelico (c. 1395–1455), shows a monk with Roman tonsure, in which the top of the head is shaved as a sign of religious devotion.

Therefore, God again is "perverse with the crooked" [Ps. 18:26], and to punish the makers of vows for their ingratitude and pride, God brings it about that they break their vows, or keep them only with prodigious labor, and remain sunk in them, never knowing the grace of faith and of baptism; that they continue in their hypocrisy to the end, since their spirit is not approved of God; and that at last they become a laughing-stock to the whole world, ever pursuing righteousness and never attaining righteousness, so that they fulfill the word of Isa. 2[:8]: "Their land is filled with idols."

I am indeed far from forbidding or discouraging anyone who may desire to vow something privately and of his own free choice; for I would not altogether despise and condemn vows. But I would most strongly advise against setting up and sanctioning the making of vows as a public mode of life. It is enough that every one should have the private right to take a vow at his own peril; but to commend the vowing of vows as a public mode of life—this I hold to be most pernicious to the church and to simple souls. First, because it runs directly counter to the Christian life, for a vow is a kind of ceremonial law and a human ordinance or presumption, from which the church has been set free through baptism; for a Christian is subject to no law but the law of God. Second, because there is no instance in Scripture of such a vow, especially of lifelong chastity, obedience, or poverty.[179] But whatever is without warrant of Scripture is most hazardous and should by no means be urged upon anyone, much less established as a common and public mode of life, even if it be permitted to somebody who wishes to make the venture at his own peril. For certain works are wrought by the Spirit in a few people, but they must not be made an example or a mode of life for all.

Moreover, I greatly fear that these votive modes of life of the religious orders belong to those things which the Apostle foretold: "They will be teaching lies in hypocrisy, forbidding marriage, and enjoining abstinence from foods which God created to be received with thanksgiving" [1 Tim. 4:2-3]. Let no one retort by pointing to SS. Bernard, Francis, Dominic,[180] and others, who founded or fostered monastic orders. Terrible and marvelous is God in his counsels toward the sons of men. He could keep Daniel, Hananiah, Azariah, and Mishael holy at the court of the king of Babylon (that is, in the midst of godlessness);[s] why could God not sanctify those men also in their perilous mode of living

179. The common threefold vow of the monastic life.

180. Bernard of Clairvaux (1090–1153) was the leading figure of the Cistercian reforms and established 163 monasteries throughout Europe. Francis of Assisi (1182–1226) founded the *Ordo Fratrum Minorum* (Order of Little Brothers), dedicated to a life of absolute poverty in order to live in conformity with Christ and his apostles. Dominic de Guzman (c. 1170–1221) was a Spanish priest who founded the *Ordo Praedicatorum* (Order of Preachers), also known as the Dominicans. A mendicant order like the Franciscans, the Dominicans were originally dedicated to the evangelization and combating heresy.

or guide them by the special operation of his Spirit, yet without desiring it to be an example to others? Besides, it is certain that none of them was saved through his vows and his religious[181] life; they were saved through faith alone, by which all people are saved, and to which that showy subservience to vows is more diametrically opposed than anything else.

But everyone may hold his or her[t] own view on this. I will return to my argument. Speaking now in behalf of the church's liberty and the glory of baptism, I feel myself in duty bound to set forth publicly the counsel I have learned under the Spirit's guidance. I therefore counsel those in high places in the churches, first of all, to abolish all those vows and religious orders, or at least not to approve and extol them. If they will not do this, then I counsel all men who would be assured of their salvation to abstain from all vows, above all from the major and lifelong vows. I give this counsel especially to teenagers and young people. This I do, first, because this manner of life has no witness or warrant in the Scriptures, as I have said, but is puffed up solely by the bulls (and they truly are "bulls"[182]) of human popes. Second, because it greatly tends to hypocrisy, by reason of its outward show and unusual character, which engender conceit and a contempt of the common Christian life. And if there were no other reason for abolishing these vows, this one would be reason enough, namely, that through them faith and baptism are slighted and works are exalted, which cannot be done without harmful results. For in the religious orders there is scarcely one in many thousands who is not more concerned about his works than about faith, and on the basis of this madness, they claim superiority over each other, as being "stricter" or "laxer," as they call it.[183]

Therefore I advise no one to enter any religious order or the priesthood; indeed, I advise everyone against it—unless he is forearmed with this knowledge and understands that the works of monks and priests, however holy and arduous they may be, do not differ one whit in the sight of God from the works of the rustic laborer in the field or the woman going about her household tasks, but that all works are measured before God by faith alone, as Jer. 5[:3] says: "O Lord, do not your eyes look for faith?"

181. The designation "religious" is technical, referring to those having formally taken monastic vows.

182. The wordplay is on *bulla*, which can also mean "bubble."

183. Monastic orders had a history of debates regarding the proper interpretation of their particular rule. Often this led to divisions within their order with stricter "observants" separating from the more lax. The most famous conflict was among the Franciscans after the death of their founder, with the stricter "Spiritualists" set in opposition to the "Conventuals." Luther himself belonged to the stricter observant branch of the Augustinians.

s   Cf. Dan. 1:6-21.

t   Feminine added.

184. Luther is referring to the Babylonian exile in the Old Testament. When King Nebuchadnezzar initiated the first deportation, he led out the upper class and aristocracy of the nation. These are the "people of captivity"—an expression taken from the Latin title to Psalm 65 (*populo transmigrationis*). Those left behind—the common folk—are the "people of the earth" (*populi terrae*); 2 Kgs. 24:14, "He carried away all Jerusalem, . . . no one remained, except the poorest people of the land."

185. E.g., Aquinas, *STh* II-II, q. 88, a. 10: "if it be decided absolutely that a particular vow is not to be observed, this is called a 'dispensation' from that vow; but if some other obligation be imposed in lieu of that which was to have been observed, the vow is said to be 'commuted.' Hence it is less to commute a vow than to dispense from a vow: both, however, are in the power of the Church."

186. Matt. 18:15-18: "If another member of the church sins against you, go and point out the fault when the two of you are alone. If the member listens to you, you have regained that one. But if you are not listened to, take one or two others along with you, so that every word may be confirmed by the evidence of two or three witnesses. If the member refuses to listen to them, tell it to the church; and if the offender refuses to listen even to the church, let such a one be to you as a Gentile and a tax collector. Truly I tell you, whatever you bind on earth will be bound in heaven, and whatever you loose on earth will be loosed in heaven."

187. Luther is referring to canon law, *Decretalium Gregorii IX,* lib. 3, tit. 34, *de*

and Sir. 32[:23]: "In all your works believe with faith in thy heart, for this is to keep the commandments of God." Indeed, the menial housework of a manservant or maidservant is often more acceptable to God than all the fastings and other works of a monk or priest, because the monk or priest lacks faith. Since, therefore, vows nowadays seem to tend only to the glorification of works and to pride, it is to be feared that there is nowhere less of faith and of the church than among the priests, monks, and bishops. These men are in truth heathen or hypocrites. They imagine themselves to be the church, or the heart of the church, the "spiritual" estate and the leaders of the church, when they are everything else but that. This is indeed "the people of the captivity," among whom all things freely given to us in baptism are held captive, while the few poor "people of the earth" who are left behind,[184] such as the married folk, appear vile in their eyes.

From what has been said we recognize two glaring errors of the Roman pontiff.

In the first place, he grants dispensation from vows,[185] and does it as if he alone of all Christians possessed this authority; so great is the temerity and audacity of wicked men. If it is possible to grant a dispensation from a vow, then any brother may grant one to his neighbor, or even to himself. But if one's neighbor cannot grant a dispensation, neither has the pope any right to do so. For where does he get this authority? From the power of the keys? But the keys belong to all, and avail only for sins, Matthew 18.[186] Now they themselves claim that vows are "of divine right." Why then does the pope deceive and destroy the poor souls of people by granting dispensations in matters of divine right, in which no dispensations can be granted? In the section, "Of vows and their redemption,"[187] he babbles indeed of having the power to change vows, just as in the law the firstborn of an ass was changed for a sheep[188] as if the firstborn of an ass, and the vow he commands to be offered everywhere and always, were one and the same thing; or as if when the Lord decrees in the law that a sheep shall be changed for an ass, the pope, a mere man, may straightway claim the same power, not in his own law, but in God's! It was not a pope, but an ass changed for a pope, that made this decretal;[189] it is so egregiously senseless and godless.

The second error is this: The pope decrees, on the other hand, that a marriage is dissolved if one party enters a monastery without the consent of the other, provided that the marriage has not yet been consummated.[190] Now I ask you, what devil puts such monstrous things into the pope's mind? God commands people to keep faith and not break their word to one another, and again, to do good with that which is their own, for God hates "robbery with a burnt offering," as is spoken by the mouth of Isaiah.[191] But spouses[u] are bound by the marriage contract to keep faith with one another, and they are not for themselves alone. They cannot break this faith by any right, and whatever they do with themselves alone is robbery, if it is done without the other's consent. Why does not those who are burdened with debt follow this same rule and obtain admission into a religious order, so as to be released from their debts and be free to break their word? O blind, blind people! Which is greater, the fidelity commanded by God or a vow devised and chosen by human beings? Are you a shepherd of souls, O pope? And you who teach these things, are you doctors of sacred theology? Why then do you teach them? No doubt because you have decked out your vow as a better work than marriage; you do not exalt faith, which alone exalts all things, but works, which are nothing in the sight of God, or which are all alike as far as merit is concerned.

I am sure, therefore, that neither human beings nor angels can grant a dispensation from vows, if they are proper vows. But I am not fully clear in my own mind whether all the things that people vow nowadays come under the head of vows. For instance, it is simply foolish and stupid for parents to dedicate their children, before birth or in infancy, to the "religious life," or to perpetual chastity;[192] indeed, it is certain that this can by no means be termed a vow. It seems to be a kind of mockery of God for them to vow things which are not at all in their power. As to the triple vow[193] of the monastic orders, the longer I consider it, the less I comprehend it, and I wonder where the custom of exacting this vow arose. Still less do I understand at what age vows may be taken in order to be legal and valid. I am pleased to find unanimous agreement that vows taken before the age of puberty are not valid.[194] Nevertheless, they deceive many young children who are ignorant both of their age and of what they are vowing. They do not observe the age of puberty in receiving such children; but the children, after making their profession, are held captive and

voto et voti redemptione, c. 7 (hereafter Decr. Greg. IX).

188. Cf. Exod. 13:13: "But every firstborn donkey you shall redeem with a sheep; if you do not redeem it, you must break its neck."

189. "Decretal" refers to papal and conciliar decrees that made up most of church law. In the broadest sense, the decretals include all official letters of the pope in which a specific decision or decree is contained. More specifically, the term refers to various collections of such decrees.

190. Decr. Greg. IX, lib. 3, tit. 32, de conversione coniugatorum, c. 2: "before the marriage is consummated one of the spouses can enter a religious order, even if the other is unwilling."

191. Isa. 61:8: "For I the LORD love justice, I hate robbery and wrongdoing [or with a burnt offering]."

192. The child dedicated to the religious life by his parents is called an "oblate." Provisions for this practice were already present in the Rule of Benedict of Nursia (c. 480–571): "let parents draw up the petition which we have mentioned above; and at the oblation let them wrap the petition and the boy's hand in the altar cloth and so offer him [to God]." Rabanus Maurus (780–856) wrote a treatise on the practice, De oblatione puerorum, arguing on the basis of biblical precedent with the redemption of the firstborn, the dedication of the Levites, and the vow of Hannah to give Samuel.

193. Poverty, chastity, and obedience.

194. According to canon law the earliest one can take a vow is age fourteen for boys and twelve for girls;

u   This sentence and what follows were singular in the original.

Decr. Greg. IX, lib. 3, tit. 31, *de regularibus et transeuntibus ad religionem*, c. 8.

consumed by a troubled conscience as though they had afterward given their consent. As if a vow which was invalid could finally become valid with the passing of the years!

It seems absurd to me that the effective date of a legitimate vow should be predetermined for others by people who cannot predetermine it for themselves. Nor do I see why a vow taken at eighteen years of age should be valid, but not one taken at ten or twelve years. It will not do to say that at eighteen a man feels his carnal desires. What if he scarcely feels them at twenty or thirty, or feels them more keenly at thirty than at twenty? Why not also set a certain age limit for the vows of poverty and obedience? But what age will you set, by which a man should feel his greed and pride, when even the most spiritual persons hardly become aware of these emotions? Therefore, no vow will ever become binding and valid until we have become spiritual, and no longer have any need of vows. You see that these are uncertain and most perilous matters, and it would therefore be a wholesome counsel to keep such lofty modes of living free of vows, and leave them to the Spirit alone as they were of old, and never in any way to change them into a mode of life which is perpetually binding.

However, let this be sufficient for the present concerning baptism and its liberty. In due time I shall perhaps discuss vows at greater length,[195] and truly there is an urgent need for this.

195. Luther would, in fact, dedicate an entire treatise to this topic in 1521 while at the Wartburg, namely, *On Monastic Vows*, LW 44:243–400.

The Sacrament of Penance

In the third place, we are to discuss the sacrament of penance. On this subject I have already given no little offense to many people by the treatises and disputations already published, in which I have amply set forth my views.[v] These I must now briefly repeat in order to unmask the tyranny that is rampant here no less than in the sacrament of the bread. For, because these two

---

v   The *Ninety-Five Theses against Indulgences* (1517), LW 31:25–33; TAL 1:13–46; *Ein Sermon von Ablaß und Gnade* (*A Sermon on Indulgences and Grace* [1517]), WA 1:239–46; TAL 1:57–66; *The Sacrament of Penance* (1519), LW 35:3–22; TAL 1:181–202; *Explanations of the Ninety-Five Theses* (1518), LW 31:83–252; *A Discussion on How Confession Should Be Made* (1520), LW 39:23–47.

sacraments furnish opportunity for gain and profit, the greed of the shepherds has raged in them with incredible zeal against the flock of Christ, although, as we have just seen in our discussion of vows, baptism too has sadly declined among adults and become the servant of greed.

The first and chief abuse of this sacrament is that they have completely abolished it. Not a vestige of the sacrament remains. For this sacrament, like the other two, consists in the word of divine promise and our faith, and they have undermined both of them. For they have adapted to their own tyranny the word of promise which Christ speaks in Matt. 16[:19] and 18[:18]: "Whatever you bind, etc.," and in the last chapter of John [20:23]: "If you forgive the sins of any, they are forgiven, etc." By these words the faith of penitents is aroused for obtaining the forgiveness of sins. But in all their writing, teaching, and preaching, their sole concern has been, not to teach what is promised to Christians in these words, or what they ought to believe, and what great consolation they might find in them, but only through force and violence to extend their own tyranny far, wide, and deep. It has finally come to such a pass that some of them have begun to command the very angels in heaven,[196] and to boast in incredible, mad wickedness that in these words they have obtained the right to rule in heaven and earth, and possess the power to bind even in heaven. Thus they say nothing of faith which is the salvation of the people, but babble only of the despotic power of the pontiffs, whereas Christ says nothing at all of power, but speaks only of faith.

In this woodcut by Albrecht Dürer (1471–1528), a man, perhaps King David, is depicted doing penance (1510).

196. The reference here is to a spurious bull of Pope Clement VI, *Ad memoriam*, promulgated during the Jubilee year of 1350. Many pilgrims traveling to Rome died from the plague that was widespread throughout Europe, and the

bull responds by saying, "We command the angels of paradise that their souls be taken directly to the bliss of paradise, as being fully absolved from purgatory." Luther seems to be referring to this event again in his *Defense and Explanation of All the Articles* (1521), LW 32:74–75: "This is what happened in the days of John Hus. In those days the pope commanded the angels in heaven to lead to heaven the souls of those pilgrims who died on the way to Rome. John Hus objected to this horrible blasphemy and more than diabolic presumption. This protest cost him his life, but he at least caused the pope to change his tune and embarrassed by this sacrilege, to refrain from such proclamation."

For Christ has not ordained authorities or powers or lordships in his church, but ministries, as we learn from the Apostle, who says: "This is how one should regard us, as ministers of Christ and stewards of the mysteries of God" [1 Cor. 4:1]. Just as, when he said: "He who believes and is baptized will be saved" [Mark 16:16], he was calling forth the faith of those who were to be baptized, so that by this word of promise a person might be certain of salvation if baptized in faith. There was no conferring of any power there, but only the instituting of the ministry of those who baptize. Similarly, here where he says, "Whatever you bind, etc." [Matt. 16:19; 18:18], he is calling forth the faith of the penitent, so that by this word of promise we[w] might be certain that if we are absolved in faith, we are truly absolved in heaven. Here there is no mention at all of power, but only of the ministry of the one who absolves. One cannot but wonder what happened to these blind and overbearing men that they did not arrogate to themselves a despotic power from the promise of baptism; or, if they did not do it there, why they presumed to do it from the promise of penance? For in both there is a like ministry, a similar promise, and the same kind of sacrament. It cannot be denied: if baptism does not belong to Peter alone, then it is a wicked usurpation of power to claim the power of the keys for the pope alone.

Again, when Christ says: "Take, this is my body, which is given for you. This is the cup in my blood, etc." [1 Cor. 11:24-25], he is calling forth the faith of those who eat, so that when their conscience has been strengthened by these words they might be certain through faith that they receive the forgiveness of sins when they have eaten. Here too, nothing is said of power, but only of the ministry.

So the promise of baptism remains to some extent, at least for infants; but the promise of the bread and the cup has been destroyed and made subservient to greed, faith has become a work, and the testament has become a sacrifice. The promise of penance, however, has been transformed into the most oppressive despotism, being used to establish a sovereignty which is more than merely temporal.

Not content with these things, *this Babylon of ours has so completely extinguished faith* that it insolently *denies its necessity in this*

---

w   The singular pronoun is replaced with the plural in this sentence.

sacrament. Indeed, with the wickedness of Antichrist it brands it as heresy for anyone to assert that faith is necessary.ˣ What more could this tyranny do than it has done? Truly, "by the waters of Babylon we sit down and weep, when we remember thee, O Zion. On the willows there we hang up our lyres" [Ps. 137:1-2]. May the Lord curse the barren willows of those streams! Amen.

Now that promise and faith have been thus blotted out and overthrown, let us see what they have put in their place. *They have divided penance into three parts—contrition, confession, and satisfaction;*ʸ but in such a way that they have removed whatever was good in each of them, and have established in each of them their caprice and tyranny.

[Contrition]

In the first place, they teach that contrition takes precedence over, and is far superior to, faith in the promise, as if contrition were not a work of faith, but a merit; indeed, they do not mention faith at all. They stick so closely to works and to those passages of Scripture where we read of many who obtained pardon by reason of their contrition and humility of heart; but they take no account of the faith which effected this contrition and sorrow of heart, as is written of the men of Nineveh in Jon. 3[:5]: "And the people of Nineveh believed God; they proclaimed a fast, etc." Others again, more bold and wicked, have invented a so-called attrition, which is converted into contrition by the power of the keys, of which they know nothing.[197] This attrition they grant to the wicked and unbelieving, and thus abolish contrition altogether. O the intolerable wrath of God, that such things should be taught in the church of Christ! Thus, with both faith and its work destroyed, we go on secure in the doctrines and opinions of men, or rather we perish in them. A contrite heart is a precious thing, but it is found only where there is an ardent faith in the promises and threats of God. Such faith, intent on the immutable truth of God, makes the conscience

197. "Attrition" is imperfect contrition, i.e., sorrow for sin for reasons less than altruistic, such as fear of punishment or love of reward. True or perfect contrition is sorrow for sin out of love for God. It is related to the traditional distinction of two kinds of "fear of God" (*timor Dei*), i.e., servile fear and filial fear. In late medieval theology, attrition was connected to the distinction of congruent merit (*meritum de congruo*—merit inadequate vis-à-vis its reward) and condign merit (*meritum de condigno*—merit intrinsically "worth" its reward). Though attrition did not fulfill the full requirements of contrition in the sacrament of penance, through the priest, God would mercifully consider it sufficient to merit grace (*meritum de congruo*), since God will not deny grace to those who do what is in them (*facere quod in se est*).

---

x   Cf. Luther's dispute with Cajetan on the role of faith, *The Proceedings at Augsburg*, LW 31:271; also TAL 1:141–42.

y   See n. 151, p. 63.

tremble, terrifies it and bruises it; and afterwards, when it is contrite, raises it up, consoles it, and preserves it. Thus the truth of God's threat is the cause of contrition, and the truth of his promise the cause of consolation, if it is believed. By such faith a man "merits" the forgiveness of sins. Therefore faith should be taught and aroused before all else. Once faith is obtained, contrition and consolation will follow inevitably of themselves.

Therefore, although there is some truth in their teaching that contrition is to be attained by the enumeration and contemplation (as they call it) of their sins,[198] yet their teaching is perilous and perverse so long as they do not teach first of all the beginnings and causes of contrition—the immutable truth of God's threat and promise which calls forth faith—so that men may learn to pay more heed to the truth of God, by which they are cast down and lifted up, than to the multitude of their sins. If their sins are regarded apart from the truth of God, they will excite afresh and increase the desire for sin rather than lead to contrition. I will say nothing now of the insurmountable task which they have imposed upon us, namely, that we are to frame a contrition for every sin. That is impossible. We can know only the smaller part of our sins; and even our good works are found to be sins, according to Ps. 143[:2]: "Enter not into judgment with your servant; for no one living is righteous before you." It is enough if we lament the sins which distress our conscience at the present moment, as well as those which we can readily call to mind. Whoever is in this frame of mind is without doubt ready to grieve and fear for all his sins, and will grieve and fear whenever they are brought to his knowledge in the future.

Beware, then, of putting your trust in your own contrition and of ascribing the forgiveness of sins to your own remorse. God does not look on you with favor because of that, but because of the faith by which you have believed God's threats and promises, and which has effected such sorrow within you. Thus we owe whatever good there may be in our penance, not to our scrupulous enumeration of sins, but to the truth of God and to our faith. All other things are the works and fruits which follow of their own accord. They do not make a person good, but are done by the one who is already made good through faith in the truth of God. Even so, "smoke goes up in his wrath; because he is angry he shakes the mountains and sets them on fire," as it is said in Ps. 18[:8, 7]). First comes the terror of this threatening, which sets

198. Cf. Aquinas, *STh* III Suppl., q. 9, a. 2: "In prescribing medicine for the body, the physician should know not only the disease for which he is prescribing, but also the general constitution of the sick person, since one disease is aggravated by the addition of another, and a medicine which would be adapted to one disease, would be harmful to another. The same is to be said in regard to sins, . . . hence it is necessary for confession that man confess all the sins that he calls to mind, and if he fails to do this, it is not a confession, but a pretense of confession."

the wicked on fire; then faith, accepting this, sends up smoke-clouds of contrition, etc.

But the trouble is not so much that contrition has been exposed to tyranny and avarice, as that it has been given over completely to wickedness and pestilent teaching. It is confession and satisfaction that have become the chief workshops of greed and power.

[Confession]

Let us first take up *confession*. There is no doubt that confession of sins is necessary and commanded of God, in Matt. 3[:6]: "They were baptized by John in the River Jordan, confessing their sins," and in 1 John 1[:9-10]: "If we confess our sins, he is faithful and just, and will forgive our sins. If we say we have not sinned, we make him a liar, and his word is not in us." If the saints may not deny their sin, how much more ought those who are guilty of great and public sins to make confession! But the institution of confession is proved most effectively of all by Matt. 18,[199] where Christ teaches that those^z who sin should be told of their faults, brought before the church, accused, and if they will not hear, be excommunicated. They "hear" if they heed the rebuke and acknowledge and confess their sins.

As to the current practice of private confession, I am heartily in favor of it, even though it cannot be proved from the Scriptures. It is useful, even necessary, and I would not have it abolished. Indeed, I rejoice that it exists in the church of Christ, for it is a cure without equal for distressed consciences. For when we have laid bare our conscience to another Christian and privately made known to the evil that lurked within, we receive from that person's lips the word of comfort [as if] spoken by God. And, if we accept this in faith, we find peace in the mercy of God speaking to us through our brother or sister. There is just one thing about it that I abominate, and that is the fact that this kind of confession has been subjected to the despotism and extortion of the pontiffs. They reserve to themselves even the secret sins,[200] and command that they be made known to confessors named by them, only to trouble the consciences of people. They merely

199. Matt. 18:15-17: "If another member of the church sins against you, go and point out the fault when the two of you are alone. If the member listens to you, you have regained that one. But if you are not listened to, take one or two others along with you, so that every word may be confirmed by the evidence of two or three witnesses. If the member refuses to listen to them, tell it to the church; and if the offender refuses to listen even to the church, let such a one be to you as a Gentile and a tax collector."

200. The notion of "reserved cases" in which the pope claimed exclusive jurisdiction to grant remission and satisfaction (*casus papales*) developed gradually as bishops would refer certain grave transgressions to the Holy See, for example, violence done to clerics and the burning of church buildings being the most common early on. Official lists of cases reserved for the pope

---

z   Plural substituted for singular in this and the next sentence.

were enumerated in the bull *In coena domini*, which was published annually against heretics since 1364. This list, however, grew with papal discretion and continued to be a contentious conflict of jurisdiction over the bishops who had claimed the right to absolve a similar list of "secret" (*casus occultus*) as well as "public" sins. In 1414, the Council of Constance tried, though unsuccessfully, to curtail these cases and leave them at the discretion of the bishop. Even the Council of Trent in 1563 would try to limit papal cases only to certain public sins, leaving the secret sins in the hands of the bishops (*Sess.* 24, *de Reform*, c. 8 and c. 20), but this, too, was often overturned by the publication of *Coena domini*.

play the pontiff, while they utterly despise the true duties of pontiffs, which are to preach the gospel and to care for the poor. Indeed, the godless despots leave the great sins to the common priests, and reserve to themselves only those sins which are of less consequence, such as those ridiculous and fictitious things in the bull *Coena domini*. To make the wickedness of their error even more apparent, they not only fail to reserve, but actually teach and approve things which are against the service of God, against faith and the chief commandments—such as their running about on pilgrimages, the perverse worship of the saints, the lying saints' legends, the various ways of trusting in works and ceremonies and practicing them. Yet in all of these faith in God is extinguished and idolatry fostered, as we see in our day. As a result we have the same kind of priests today as Jeroboam ordained of old in Dan and Beersheba, ministers of the golden calves,[a] men who are ignorant of the law of God, of faith, and of whatever pertains to the feeding of Christ's sheep. They inculcate in the people nothing but their own inventions with fear and violence.

Although I urge that this outrage of reserved cases should be borne patiently, even as Christ bids us bear all human tyranny, and teaches us that we should obey these extortioners; nevertheless, I deny that they have the right to make such reservations, and I do not believe that they can bring one jot or tittle of proof that they have it. But I am going to prove the contrary. In the first place, Christ speaks in Matt. 18 of public sins and says that if our brother hears us, when we tell him his fault, we have saved the soul of our brother, and that he is to be brought before the church only if he refuses to hear us, so that his sin can be corrected among brethren.[b] How much more will it be true of secret sins, that they are forgiven if one brother freely makes confession to another? So it is not necessary to tell it to the church, that is, as these babblers interpret it, to the prelate or priest. On this matter we have further authority from Christ, where he says in the same chapter: "Whatever you bind on earth shall be bound in heaven, and whatever you loose on earth shall be loosed in heaven" [Matt. 18:18]. For this is said to each and every Christian. Again, he says in the same place: "Again I say to you, if two

a   1 Kgs. 12:26-32.
b   Matt. 18:15-17.

of you agree on earth about anything they ask, it will be done for them by my father in heaven" [Matt. 18:19]. Now, the one who lays secret sins before another believer and craves pardon, certainly agrees with this brother or sister on earth, in the truth which is Christ. Of this Christ says even more clearly, confirming his preceding words: "For truly, I say to you, where two or three are gathered in my name, there am I in the midst of them" [Matt. 18:20].

Hence, I have no doubt but that we are absolved from our secret sins when we have made confession, privately before any brother or sister, either of our own accord or after being rebuked, and have sought pardon and amended our ways, no matter how much the violence of the pontiffs may rage against it. For Christ has given to every one of his believers the power to absolve even open sins. Add yet this little point: If any reservation of secret sins were valid, so that one could not be saved unless they were forgiven, then one's salvation would be prevented most of all by those aforementioned good works and idolatries that are taught by the popes nowadays. But if these most grievous sins do not prevent one's salvation, how foolish it is to reserve those lighter sins! In truth, it is the foolishness and blindness of the shepherds that produce these monstrous things in the church. Therefore I would admonish those princes of Babylon and bishops of Beth-aven[201] to refrain from reserving any cases whatsoever. Let them, moreover, permit all brothers and sisters most freely to hear the confession of secret sins, so that the sinner may make his sins known to whomever he will and seek pardon and comfort, that is, the word of Christ, by the mouth of his neighbor. For with these presumptions of theirs they only ensnare the consciences of the weak without necessity, establish their wicked despotism, and fatten their avarice on the sins and ruin of their brethren. Thus they stain their hands with the blood of souls; sons are devoured by their parents. Ephraim devours Judah, and Syria Israel, with an open mouth, as Isaiah says.[202]

To these evils they have added the "circumstances,"[c] and also the mothers, daughters, sisters, sisters-in-law, branches and fruits of sins; since these most astute and idle men have worked out, if you please, a kind of family tree of relationships and

201. Hos. 4:15; 10:5. "Beth-aven" was the new name given to Bethel by the prophet in response to Israel's idolatry. Rather than "house of God," it was "house of nothingness."

202. Isa. 9:20-22: "They gorged on the right, but still were hungry, and they devoured on the left, but were not satisfied; they devoured the flesh of their own kindred; Manasseh devoured Ephraim, and Ephraim Manasseh, and together they were against Judah. For all this his anger has not turned away; his hand is stretched out still."

c   See n. 154, p. 64.

affinities even among sins—so prolific is wickedness coupled with ignorance. For this conception, whatever rogue may be its author, has become a public law, like many others. Thus do the shepherds keep watch over the church of Christ: whatever new work or superstition those most stupid devotees may have dreamed of, they immediately drag to the light of day, deck out with indulgences, and fortify with bulls. So far are they from suppressing such things and preserving for God's people true faith and liberty. For what has our liberty to do with the tyranny of Babylon?

My advice would be to ignore all "circumstances" whatsoever. With Christians there is only one circumstance—that a fellow Christian[d] has sinned. For there is no person to be compared with a fellow Christian. And the observance of places, times, days, persons, and all other rank superstition only magnifies the things that are nothing, to the injury of the things which are everything; as if anything could be of greater weight or importance than the glory of Christian fellowship! Thus they bind us to places, days, and persons, so that the name of [Christian] "brother" [or "sister"] loses its value, and we serve in bondage instead of being free—we, to whom all days, places, persons, and all external things are one and the same.

[Satisfaction]

How unworthily they have dealt with *satisfaction,* I have abundantly shown in the controversies concerning indulgences.[e] They have grossly abused it, to the ruin of Christians in body and soul. To begin with, they have taught it in such a manner that the people have never had the slightest understanding what satisfaction really is, namely, the renewal of one's life. Then, they so continually harp on it and emphasize its necessity, that they leave no room for faith in Christ. With these scruples they torture poor consciences to death; and one runs to Rome, one to this place, another to that; this one to Chartreuse,[203] that one to some other place; one scourges himself with rods, another mortifies his body with fasts and vigils; and all cry with the same

203. The founding cloister of the Carthusian order, founded by Bruno of Cologne (1030–1101) in 1084.

---

d   *Brother* in the German.

e   Cf. *A Sermon on Indulgence and Grace* (1518), WA 1:243–46; TAL 1:56–65; *Resolutiones* (1518), concl. 5., WA 1:538,1–35.

mad zeal: "Lo, here is Christ! Lo, there!" believing that the kingdom of Christ, which is within us, will come with observation.[204]

For these monstrous things we are indebted to you, O Roman See, and to your murderous laws and ceremonies, with which you have corrupted all humankind, so that they believe they can with works make satisfaction for sin to God, when God can be satisfied only by the faith of a contrite heart! Not only do you keep this faith silent with this uproar of yours, but you even oppress it, only so that your insatiable bloodsucker may have those to whom it may say, "Give, give!" [Prov. 30:15] and may traffic in sins.

Some have gone even further and have constructed those instruments for driving souls to despair, their decrees that the penitents must rehearse all sins anew for which they neglected to make the imposed satisfaction. What would they not venture to do, these men who were born for the sole purpose of carrying all things into a tenfold captivity?

Moreover, how many, I ask, are possessed with the notion that they are in a saved state and are making satisfaction for their sins, if they only mumble over, word for word, the prayers imposed by the priest, even though meanwhile they never give a thought to the amending of their way of life! They believe that their life is changed in the one moment of contrition and confession, and there remains only to make satisfaction for their past sins. How should they know better if they have not been taught otherwise? No thought is given here to the mortifying of the flesh, no value is attached to the example of Christ, who, when he absolved the woman caught in adultery, said: "Go, and do not sin again" [John 8:11], thereby laying upon her the cross, that is, the mortifying of her flesh. This perverse error is greatly encouraged by the fact that we absolve sinners before the satisfaction has

This image by an unknown artist depicts flagellants doing penance.

204. Cf. Luke 17:20f.: "The kingdom of God is not coming with things that can be observed; nor will they say, 'Look, here it is!' or 'There it is!' For, in fact, the kingdom of God is among you." Luther's wordplay is on "observation" (*observantia*), which can also refer to the monastic observants; see n. 183, p. 81.

been completed, so that they are more concerned about completing the satisfaction, which is a lasting thing, than they are about contrition, which they suppose to be over and done with when they have made confession. Absolution ought rather to follow on the completion of satisfaction, as it did in the early church, with the result that, after completing the work, penitents gave themselves with much greater diligence to faith and the living of a new life.

But this must suffice in repetition of what I have said more fully in connection with indulgences, and *in general this must suffice for the present concerning the three sacraments*, which have been treated, and yet not treated, in so many harmful books on the *Sentences*[f] and on the laws. It remains to attempt some discussion of the other "sacraments" also, lest I seem to have rejected them without cause.

Confirmation

It is amazing that it should have entered the minds of these men to make a sacrament of confirmation out of the laying on of hands. We read that Christ touched the little children in that way,[g] and that by it the apostles imparted the Holy Spirit,[h] ordained presbyters,[i] and cured the sick;[j] as the Apostle writes to Timothy: "Do not be hasty in the laying on of hands" [1 Tim. 5:22]. Why have they not also made a "confirmation" out of the sacrament of the bread? For it is written in Acts 9[:19]: "And he took food and was strengthened," and in Ps. 104[:15]: "And bread to strengthen man's heart." Confirmation would thus include three sacraments—the bread, ordination, and confirmation itself. But if everything the apostles did is a sacrament, why have they not rather made preaching a sacrament?

205. Confirmation was seen in connection with the gift of the Holy Spirit through apostolic laying on of hands (e.g., Acts 8:15f.) in the context of baptism. Alternatively, the sacrament has also been called chrism, especially in the Eastern church; in reference to the anointing of the Spirit it also was accompanied by the anointing of oil. Because of its origination with the apostles, confirmation was, like ordination, a sacramental act performed by the bishop. Cf., for example, Aquinas, *STh* III, q. 72, a. 11: "the conferring of this sacrament is reserved to bishops, who possess supreme power in the Church: just as in the primitive Church, the fullness of the Holy Ghost was given by the apostles, in whose place the bishops stand (Acts 8). Hence Pope Urban I (r. 222–230) says: "All the faithful should, after baptism, receive the Holy Ghost by the imposition of the bishop's hand, that they may become perfect Christians."

f   See n. 56, p. 30.
g   Mark 10:16.
h   Acts 8:17; 19:6.
i   Acts 6:6.
j   Mark 16:18.

I do not say this because I condemn the seven sacraments, but because I deny that they can be proved from the Scriptures. Would that there were in the church such a laying on of hands as there was in apostolic times, whether we chose to call it confirmation or healing! But there is nothing left of it now but what we ourselves have invented to adorn the office of bishops,[205] that they may not be entirely without work in the church. For after they relinquished to their inferiors those arduous sacraments together with the Word as being beneath their attention (since whatever the divine majesty has instituted they seem to need to despise!) it was no more than right that we should discover something easy and not too burdensome for such delicate and great heroes to do, and should by no means entrust it to the lower clergy as something common, for whatever human wisdom has decreed must be held in honor among all! Therefore, as the priests are, so let their ministry and duty be. For a bishop who does not preach the gospel or practice the cure of souls—what is he but an idol in the world [1 Cor. 8:4], who has nothing but the name and appearance of a bishop?

A woodcut of the seven sacraments of the Roman Catholic Church adorns the title page of this sermon on baptism (Leipzig, 1520) by Luther. The scene depicting the sacrament of confirmation is the center image on the left.

But *instead of this we seek sacraments that have been divinely instituted, and among these we see no reason for numbering confirmation.* For to constitute a sacrament there must be above all things else a word of divine promise, by which faith may be exercised. But we read nowhere that Christ ever gave a promise concerning confirmation, although he laid hands on many and included the laying on of hands among the signs in the last chapter of Mark [16:18]:

206. The Scripture most often cited in connected with marriage is Eph. 5:22-32, especially "the two will become one flesh. This is a great mystery . . . [Lat. *sacramentum*]." The sacramental character of marriage is articulated in the tradition in a variety of sources, though what constitutes a sacrament varied. For example, Augustine, in his work *On the Good of Marriage* (401), c. 32, notes the following: "Among all nations and all people the good that is secured by marriage consists in the offspring and in the chastity of married fidelity; but, in the case of God's people, it consists moreover in the holiness of the sacrament, by reason of which it is forbidden, even after a separation has taken place, to marry another as long as the first partner lives . . . just as priests are ordained to draw together a Christian community, and even though no such community be formed, the sacrament of orders still abides in those ordained, or just as the sacrament of the Lord, once it is conferred, abides even in one who is dismissed from his office on account of guilt, although in such a one it abides unto judgment." Peter Lombard lists marriage as one of the seven sacraments, noting that it offers only a remedy against sin rather than any helping grace, *Sentences* 4, d. 2, c. 1. In 1139, the Second Lateran Council assigned marriage along with the Eucharist and baptism as priestly acts, and at the Council of Verona, in 1184, marriage was designated as a sacrament.

207. "New Law" (*nova lex*) is a traditional designation for the gospel and the New Testament, set in contrast to the "Old Law" (*vetus lex*), i.e., the law of Moses.

"They will lay their hands on the sick; and they will recover." Yet no one has applied this to a sacrament, for that is not possible.

For this reason it is sufficient to regard confirmation as a certain churchly rite or sacramental ceremony, similar to other ceremonies, such as the blessing of water and the like. For if every other creature is sanctified by the Word and by prayer,[k] why should not we much rather be sanctified by the same means? Still, these things cannot be called sacraments of faith, because they have no divine promise connected with them, neither do they save; but the sacraments do save those who believe the divine promise.

Marriage

[Marriage Is Not a Sacrament]

Not only is marriage regarded as a sacrament without the least warrant of Scripture,[206] but the very ordinances that extol it as a sacrament have turned it into a farce. Let us look into this a little.

We have said that in every sacrament there is a word of divine promise, to be believed by whoever receives the sign, and that the sign alone cannot be a sacrament. Nowhere do we read that the man who marries a wife receives any grace of God. There is not even a divinely instituted sign in marriage, nor do we read anywhere that marriage was instituted by God to be a sign of anything. To be sure, whatever takes place in a visible manner can be understood as a figure or allegory of something invisible. But figures or allegories are not sacraments, in the sense in which we use the term.

Furthermore, since marriage has existed from the beginning of the world and is still found among unbelievers, there is no reason why it should be called a sacrament of the New Law[207] and of the church alone. The marriages of the ancients were no less sacred than are ours, nor are those of unbelievers less true marriages than those of believers, and yet they are not regarded as sacraments. Besides, even among believers there are married folk who are wicked and worse than any heathen; why should marriage be called a sacrament in their case and not among

---

k   1 Tim. 4:4-5.

A marriage ceremony presided over by a priest,
depicted in a 1522 publication.

the heathen? Or are we going to talk the same sort of nonsense
about baptism and the church and say that marriage is a sacrament only in the church, just as some make the mad claim that
temporal power exists only in the church? That is childish and
foolish talk, by which we expose our ignorance and foolhardi-
ness to the ridicule of unbelievers.

But they will say, "The Apostle says in Eph. 5[:31-32], 'The
two shall become one. This is a great sacrament.' Surely you are
not going to contradict so plain a statement of the Apostle!" I
reply: This argument like the others betrays great shallowness
and a careless and thoughtless reading of Scripture. Nowhere
in all of the Holy Scriptures is this word *sacramentum* employed
in the sense in which we use the term; it has an entirely different meaning. For wherever it occurs it denotes not the sign of
a sacred thing,[208] but the sacred, secret, hidden thing itself.[209]

208. Cf. Augustine, *The City of God* 10,
5: "a sacrament, that is, a sacred sign";
Lombard, *Sentences* 4, d. 1,
c. 2: "A sacrament is a sign of a sacred
thing"; Aquinas, *STh* III, q. 60, a. 3:
"a sacrament properly speaking is
that which is ordained to signify our
sanctification. In which three things
may be considered; viz. the very cause
of our sanctification, which is Christ's
passion; the form of our sanctification,
which is grace and the virtues; and
the ultimate end of our sanctification,
which is eternal life. And all these are
signified by the sacraments."

209. Cf. Aquinas, *STh* III, q. 60, a. 1:
"a thing may be called a 'sacrament,'
either from having a certain hidden
sanctity, and in this sense a sacrament
is a 'sacred secret'; or from having some
relationship to this sanctity, which
relationship may be that of a cause, or
of a sign or of any other relation. But
now we are speaking of sacraments in a
special sense, as implying the habitude
of sign: and in this way a sacrament is a
kind of sign."

210. The common Latin translation of "mystery" (Gk.: *mysterion*) in the Vulgate Bible is *sacramentum*, though there are instances in which it retains a Latinized form of the original, i.e., *mysterium*.

211. In his Romans lectures (1515-16), Luther began to realize certain incompatibilities with the way the Scholastic tradition used and defined theological words and the manner in which Paul used them. Repeatedly he noted that there was a stark contrast between the way in which the apostle speaks (*modus loquendi apostoli*) and the way the Scholastics talked (*modus loquendi philosophiae . . . Aristoteli*). Exasperated, he famously wrote in his notes, "O pig-theologians . . . O ignorance of sin! O ignorance of God! O ignorance of the law!" In his 1522 translation of the New Testament, he included in his preface to Romans a list of biblical vocabulary that had been misinterpreted by the Scholastics, providing his own definitions for such key words as *law, sin, grace, faith, righteousness, flesh,* and *spirit.* See Leif Grane, *Modus Loquendi Theologicus: Luthers Kampf um die Erneuerung der Theologie 1515–1518*, Acta Theologica Danica, vol. 12 (Leiden: Brill, 1975).

212. 1 Cor. 2:7-8: "But we speak God's wisdom, secret and hidden, which God decreed before the ages for our glory. None of the rulers of this age understood this; for if they had, they would not have crucified the Lord of glory."

213. 1 Cor. 1:22-24: "For Jews demand signs and Greeks desire wisdom, but we proclaim Christ crucified, a stumbling block to Jews and foolishness to Gentiles, but to those who are the called, both Jews and Greeks, Christ the

Thus Paul writes in 1 Cor. 4[:1]: "This is how one should regard us, as servants of Christ and stewards of the 'mysteries' of God," that is, the sacraments. For where we have the word *sacramentum* the Greek original has *mysterion*, which the translator sometimes translates and sometimes retains in its Greek form.[210] Thus our verse in the Greek reads: "They two shall become one. This is a great mystery." This explains how they came to understand a sacrament of the New Law here, a thing they would never have done if they had read *mysterium*, as it is in the Greek.

Thus Christ himself is called a "sacrament" in 1 Tim. 3[:16]: "Great indeed, is the sacrament (that is, the mystery): He was manifested in the flesh, vindicated in the Spirit, seen by angels, preached among the nations, believed on in the world, taken up in glory." Why have they not drawn out of this passage an eighth sacrament of the New Law, since they have the clear authority of Paul? But if they restrained themselves here, where they had a most excellent opportunity to invent new sacraments, why are they so unrestrained in the other passage? Plainly, it was their ignorance of both words and things that betrayed them. They clung to the mere sound of the words, indeed, to their own fancies. For, having once arbitrarily taken the word *sacramentum* to mean a sign, they immediately, without thought or scruple, made a "sign" of it every time they came upon it in the Holy Scriptures. Such new meanings of words, human customs, and other things they have dragged into the Holy Scriptures. They have transformed the Scriptures according to their own dreams, making anything out of any passage whatsoever. Thus they continually chatter nonsense about the terms: good work, evil work, sin, grace, righteousness, virtue, and almost all the fundamental words and things.[211] For they employ them all after their own arbitrary judgment, learned from the writings of men, to the detriment of both the truth of God and of our salvation.

Therefore, sacrament, or mystery, in Paul is that wisdom of the Spirit, hidden in a mystery, as he says in 1 Cor. 2, which is Christ, who for this very reason is not known to the rulers of this world, wherefore they also crucified him,[212] and for them he remains to this day folly, an offense, a stumbling stone,[213] and a sign that is spoken against.[214] The preachers he calls stewards of these mysteries[215] because they preach Christ, the power and the wisdom of God,[l] yet in such a way that, unless you believe, you cannot understand it. Therefore, a sacrament is a mystery, or secret thing, which is set forth in words, but received by the faith of the heart. Such a sacrament is spoken of in the passage before us: "The two shall become one. This is a great sacrament,"[m] which they understand as spoken of marriage,[216] whereas Paul himself wrote these words as applying to Christ and the church, and clearly explained them himself by saying: "I take it to mean Christ and the church" [Eph. 5:32]. See how well Paul and these men agree! Paul says he is proclaiming a great sacrament in Christ and the church, but they proclaim it in terms of man and a woman! If such liberty in the interpretation of the sacred Scriptures is permitted, it is small wonder that one finds here anything one pleases, even a hundred sacraments.

Christ and the church are, therefore, a mystery, that is, a great and secret thing which can and ought to be represented in terms of marriage as a kind of outward allegory. But marriage ought not for that reason to be called a sacrament. The heavens are a type of the apostles, as Ps. 19 declares; the sun is a type of Christ; the waters, of the peoples; but that does not make those things sacraments, for in every case there are lacking both the divine institution and the divine promise, which constitute a sacrament.[217] Hence Paul, in Ephesians 5, following his own mind, applies to Christ these words of Genesis 2 about marriage;[n] or else, following the general view, he teaches that the spiritual marriage of Christ is also contained therein, when he says: "As Christ cherishes the church, because we are members of his body, of his flesh and his bones. 'For this reason a man shall leave his father and mother and be joined to his wife, and the two shall become one.' This is a great sacrament, and I take it to mean Christ and the church." You see, he would have the whole passage apply to Christ, and is at pains to admonish the reader to understand that the sacrament is in Christ and the church, not in marriage.[o]

power of God and the wisdom of God." Cf. Rom. 9:32-33.

214. Luke 2:34: "Then Simeon blessed them and said to his mother Mary, 'This child is destined for the falling and the rising of many in Israel, and to be a sign that will be opposed.'"

215. 1 Cor. 4:1: "Think of us in this way, as servants of Christ and stewards of God's mysteries."

216. Lombard, *Sentences* 4, d. 26, c. 6: "since marriage is a sacrament, it is both a sacred sign and the sign of a sacred thing, namely of joining of Christ and the Church, as the Apostle says. . . . For just as there is between the partners to a marriage a joining according to the consent of souls and the intermingling of bodies, so the Church joins herself to Christ by will and nature." Aquinas, *STh* III Suppl., q. 42, a. 1.

217. Ps. 19:2-5: "The heavens are telling the glory of God; and the firmament proclaims his handiwork. . . . In the heavens he has set a tent for the sun, which comes out like a bridegroom from his wedding canopy." Luther's interpretation, which reflects the traditional allegorical interpretation of this Psalm in the history of exegesis, is first set forth in his lectures on the Psalms in 1513: *"the heavens tell,* [i.e.] the apostles and evangelists . . . *and the firmament proclaims,* [i.e.] the apostolic church . . . full of stars, i.e., the saints. . . . *for the sun,* in Christ . . . *he sets,* God . . . *his tabernacle,* his church" (WA 55/I:160; emphasis mine).

---

l 1 Cor. 1:24.

m Eph. 5:31-32.

n Gen. 2:24.

o At this point comes a paragraph that clearly breaks the flow of thought, though it is not clear how this might fit under Luther's treatment of penance earlier. It seems to have been an accidental

Granted that marriage is a figure of Christ and the church; yet it is not a divinely instituted sacrament, but invented by those in the church who are carried away by their ignorance of both the word and the thing. This ignorance, when it does not conflict with the faith, is to be borne in charity, just as many other human practices due to weakness and ignorance are borne in the church, so long as they do not conflict with the faith and the Holy Scriptures. But we are now arguing for the certainty and purity of faith and the Scriptures. We expose our faith to ridicule if we affirm that a certain thing is contained in the sacred Scriptures and in the articles of our faith, only to be refuted and shown that it is not contained in them; being found ignorant of our own affairs, we become a stumbling block to our opponents and to the weak. But most of all we should guard against impairing the authority of the Holy Scriptures. For those things which have been delivered to us by God in the sacred Scriptures must be sharply distinguished from those that have been invented by men in the church, no matter how eminent they may be for saintliness and scholarship.

So far concerning marriage itself.

insertion by the printer. The paragraph is reproduced here as a note for reference.

> I admit, of course, that the sacrament of penance existed in the Old Law, and even from the beginning of the world. But the new promise of penance and the gift of the keys are peculiar to the New Law. Just as we now have baptism instead of circumcision, so we have the keys instead of sacrifices and other signs of penance. We said above that the same God at various times gave different promises and diverse signs for the remission of sins and the salvation of men; nevertheless, all received the same. Thus it is said in 2 Cor. 4[:13], "Since we have the same spirit of faith, we too believe, and so we speak." And in 1 Cor. 10, "Our fathers all ate the same supernatural food and drank the same supernatural drink. For they drank from the supernatural Rock which followed them, and the Rock was Christ." Thus also in Heb. 11, "They all died, not having received what was promised, since God had foreseen something better for us, that apart from us they should not be made perfect." For Christ himself is, yesterday and today and forever the head of his church, from the beginning even to the end of the world. Therefore there are diverse signs, but the faith of all is the same. Indeed, without faith it is impossible to please God, yet by it Abel did please him.

p   Cf. Gen. 10:8f. See n. 13, p. 15.

[Canonical Impediments to Marriage]

But what shall we say concerning the wicked laws of men by which this divinely ordained way of life has been ensnared and tossed to and fro? Good God! It is dreadful to contemplate the audacity of the Roman despots, who both dissolve and compel marriages as they please. I ask you, has humankind been handed over to the caprice of these men for them to mock them and in every way abuse them and make of them whatever they please, for the sake of filthy lucre?

There is circulating far and wide and enjoying a great reputation a book whose contents have been confusedly poured together out of all the dregs and filth of human ordinances. Its title is "The Angelic *Summa*,"[218] although it ought rather to be "The More than Devilish *Summa*." Among endless other monstrosities, which are supposed to instruct the confessors, whereas they most mischievously confuse them, there are enumerated in this book eighteen impediments to marriage. If you will examine these with the just and unprejudiced eye of faith, you will see that they belong to those things which the Apostle foretold: "There shall be those that give heed to the spirits of demons, speaking lies in hypocrisy, forbidding to marry" [1 Tim. 4:1-3]. What is "forbidding to marry" if it is not this—to invent all those hindrances and set those snares, in order to prevent people from marrying, or, if they are married to annul their marriage? Who gave this power to men? Granted that they were holy men and impelled by godly zeal, why should another's holiness disturb my liberty? Why should another's zeal take me captive? Let whoever will be a saint and a zealot, and to his heart's content, only let him not bring harm upon another, and let him not rob me of my liberty!

Yet I am glad that those shameful laws have at last reached their full measure of glory, which is this: that the Romanists of our day have through them become merchants. What is it that they sell? Vulvas and penises—merchandise indeed most worthy of such merchants, grown altogether filthy and obscene through greed and godlessness. For there is no impediment nowadays that may not be legalized through the intercession of mammon. These laws of men seem to have sprung into existence for the sole purpose of serving those greedy men and rapacious Nimrods[p] as snares for taking money and as nets for catching souls, and in

218. A fifteenth-century handbook on casuistry, the *Summa de casibus conscientiae* was popularly named after its author, Angelo Carletti di Chiviasso (1411-1495), and often used by priests as a guide to hearing confession. In the section on "Matrimony," the book listed eighteen impediments to marriage.

order that "abomination" might stand in "the holy place" [Matt. 24:15], the church of God, and openly sell to people the privy parts of both sexes, or (as the Scriptures say) "shame and nakedness,"[q] of which they had previously robbed them by means of their laws. O worthy trade for our pontiffs to ply, instead of the ministry of the gospel, which in their greed and pride they despise, being given up to a reprobate mind[r] with utter shame and infamy.

But what shall I say or do? If I enter into details, the treatise will grow beyond all bounds. Everything is in such dire confusion that one does not know where to begin, how far to go, and where to leave off. This I do know, that no state is governed successfully by means of laws. If rulers are wise, they[s] will govern better by a natural sense of justice than by laws. If they are not wise, they will foster nothing but evil through legislation, since they will not know what use to make of the laws nor how to adapt them to the case at hand. Therefore, in civil affairs more stress should be laid on putting good and wise leaders in office than on making laws; for such leaders will themselves be the very best of laws, and will judge every variety of ease with a lively sense of equity. And if there is knowledge of the divine law combined with natural wisdom, then written laws will be entirely superfluous and harmful. Above all, love needs no laws whatever.[219]

Nevertheless, I will say and do what I can. I ask and urge all priests and friars when they encounter any impediment to marriage from which the pope can grant dispensation but which is not stated in the Scriptures, by all means to confirm[220] all marriages that may have been contracted in any way[221] contrary to the ecclesiastical or pontifical laws. But let them arm themselves with the divine law which says: "What God has joined together, let no man put asunder" [Matt. 19:6]. For the joining together of a man and a woman is of divine law and is binding, however much it may conflict with the laws of men; the laws of men must give way before it without any hesitation. For if a man leaves father and mother and cleaves to his wife,[t] how much more will he tread underfoot the silly and wicked laws of men, in order to

219. Luther's outspoken judgments about human institutions in this paragraph and elsewhere were evidently perceived as too radical and unreasonable. In the first editions of Luther's collected works, both the Wittenberg and Jena editions, this paragraph is entirely deleted.

220. Namely, by officiating the marriage ceremony.

221. Marriages were "contracted" by betrothal and most often arranged by parents. The secret engagement of young people without parental consent presented a problem at this time because marriage was often used to advance the family's fortunes. Many medieval theologians concluded that consent between two people constituted a valid marriage. Luther disagreed, but also encouraged both parents and children to deal with each other in a loving way. See *That Parents Should Neither Compel nor Hinder Marriage . . .* (1524), LW 45:385–93. Also, for apparently the same reasons as the previous paragraph, "in any way" (*quoquo modo*) is deleted from the Wittenberg and Jena editions of Luther's works.

q   Cf. Lev. 18:6-18.

r   Rom. 1:28.

s   The male singular pronoun is replaced by the plural in this sentence.

t   Matt. 19:5.

cleave to his wife! And if pope, bishop, or official[222] should annul any marriage because it was contracted contrary to the laws of men, he is Antichrist, he does violence to nature, and is guilty of treason against the Divine Majesty, because this word stands: "What God has joined together, let no man put asunder" [Matt. 19:6].

Besides this, no human being had the right to frame such laws, and Christ has granted to Christians a liberty which is above all human laws, especially where a law of God conflicts with them. Thus it is said in Mark 2[:28]: "The Son of man is lord even of the Sabbath," and "Humankind was not made for the Sabbath, but the Sabbath for humankind" [Mark 2:27]. Moreover, such laws were condemned beforehand by Paul when he foretold that there would be those who forbid marriage.[223] Here, therefore, those inflexible impediments derived from affinity,*u* by spiritual or legal relationship, and from blood relationship must give way, so far as the Scriptures permit, in which the second degree of consanguinity alone is prohibited. Thus it is written in Lev. 18[:6-18], where there are twelve persons a man is prohibited from marrying: his mother, stepmother, full sister, half-sister by either parent, granddaughter, father's or mother's sister, daughter-in-law, brother's wife, wife's sister, stepdaughter, and his uncle's wife. Here only the first degree of affinity and the second degree of consanguinity are forbidden; yet not without exception, as will appear on closer examination, for the brother's or sister's daughter—the niece—is not included in the prohibition, although she is in the second degree.[224] Therefore, if a marriage has been contracted outside of these degrees, which are the only ones that have been prohibited by God's appointment, it should by no means be annulled on account of human laws. For marriage itself, being a divine institution, is incomparably superior to any laws, so that marriage should not be annulled for the sake of the law, rather the laws should be broken for the sake of marriage.

In the same way that nonsense about compaternities, commaternities, confraternities, consororities, and confilieties[225] must be completely abolished in the contracting of marriage.

222. The judge in the episcopal court.

223. 1 Tim. 4:1-3: "Now the Spirit expressly says that in later times some will renounce the faith by paying attention to deceitful spirits and teachings of demons, through the hypocrisy of liars whose consciences are seared with a hot iron. They forbid marriage and demand abstinence from foods, which God created to be received with thanksgiving by those who believe and know the truth."

224. The word *consanguinity* refers to kinship ties, while *affinity* refers to those who are related by marriage.

225. Relationships arising from sponsorship at baptism or through legal adoption.

u   The Wittenberg and Jena editions delete this section from here to the end of the paragraph. See n. 219, p. 102.

What was it but superstition that invented this "spiritual affinity"? If one who baptized is not permitted to marry her whom he has baptized or stood sponsor for, what right has any Christian man to marry a Christian woman? Is the relationship that grows out of the external rite or sign of the sacrament more intimate than that which grows out of the blessing of the sacrament itself? Is not a Christian man the brother of a Christian woman, and is she not his sister? Is not a baptized man the spiritual brother of a baptized woman? How foolish we are! If a man instructs his wife in the gospel and in faith in Christ, does he not truly become her father in Christ? And is it not lawful for her to remain his wife? Would not Paul have had the right to marry a girl from among the Corinthians, of whom he boasts that he became their father in Christ?[v] See then, how Christian liberty has been suppressed through the blindness of human superstition.

There is even less in the "legal affinity," and yet they have set it above the divine right of marriage.[w] Nor would I agree to that impediment which they call "disparity of religion,"[x] which forbids one to marry an unbaptized person, either simply, or on condition that she be converted to the faith. Who made this prohibition? God or human beings? Who gave human beings the power to prohibit such a marriage? Indeed, the spirits that speak lies in hypocrisy, as Paul says.[y] Of them it must be said: "Godless men have told me fables which do not conform to your law" [Ps. 119:85].[226] The heathen Patricius married the Christian Monica, mother of St. Augustine;[z] why should that not be permitted today? The same stupid, or rather, wicked severity is seen in the "impediment of crime," as when a man has married a woman with whom he previously had committed adultery, or when he plotted to bring about the death of a woman's husband in order to be able to wed the widow.[a] I ask you, whence comes this cruelty of person toward person, which even God never demanded?

226. Luther is quoting the Latin Vulgate version of this psalm (118 in the Vulgate), which does not conform to modern English translations.

v   1 Cor. 4:15.

w   The first sentence is also missing from the Wittenberg and Jena editions; see n. 219, p. 102.

x   Cf. Aquinas, *STh* III Suppl., q. 59, "On the Disparity of Worship as an Impediment to Marriage."

y   1 Tim. 4:2.

z   Cf. Augustine, *Confessions* 9, 9, 19.

a   Cf. *Decr. Greg. IX*, lib. 4, tit. 7.

Do they pretend not to know that Bathsheba, the wife of Uriah, was wed by David, a most saintly man, after the double crime of adultery and murder?[b] If the divine law did this, what are these despotic men doing to their fellow servants?

They[c] also recognize what they call "the impediment of a tie," that is, when a man is bound to another woman by betrothal. Here they conclude that, if he has had sexual relations with a second woman, his engagement to the first becomes null and void. This I do not understand at all. I hold that he who has betrothed himself to one woman no longer belongs to himself. Because of this fact, by the prohibition of the divine law, he belongs to the first with whom he has not had intercourse, even though he has had intercourse with the second. For it was not in his power to give the latter what was no longer his own; he has deceived her and actually committed adultery. But they regard the matter differently because they pay more heed to the carnal union than to the divine command, according to which the man, having made a promise to the first woman, should keep it always. For whoever would give anything must give of that which is his own. And God forbids us to transgress and wrong a brother or sister in any matter.[d] This must be observed over and above all human ordinances.. Therefore I believe that such a man cannot with a good conscience live in marriage with a second woman, and this impediment should be completely reversed. For if a monastic vow makes a man no longer his own, why does not a pledge of mutual faithfulness do the same? After all, faithfulness is one of the precepts and fruits of the Spirit, in Gal. 5:[22], while a monastic vow is of human invention. And if a wife may claim her husband back, despite the fact that he has taken a monastic vow, why may not an engaged woman claim back her betrothed, even though he has intercourse with another? But we have said above that he who has promised to marry a girl may not take a monastic vow, but is in duty bound to marry her because he is in duty bound to keep faith with her; and this faith he may not break for any human ordinance, because it is commanded

---

b   2 Sam. 11:1-27.

c   This entire paragraph is missing from the Wittenberg and Jena editions; see n. 219, p. 102.

d   1 Thess. 4:6.

227. Luther sarcastically pits one impediment against the other. Normally, the "impediment of error" has to do with mistaken identity. See Aquinas, *STh* III Suppl., q. 51, a. 2: "Wherefore error, in order to void marriage, must needs be about the essentials of marriage. Now marriage includes two things, namely the two persons who are joined together, and the mutual power over one another wherein marriage consists. The first of these is removed by error concerning the person, the second by error regarding the condition, since a slave cannot freely give power over his body to another, without his master's consent. For this reason these two errors, and no others, are an impediment to matrimony."

228. Cf. Aquinas, *STh* III Suppl., q. 53, a. 3: "Hence among the Greeks and other Eastern peoples a sacred order is an impediment to the contracting of matrimony but it does not forbid the use of marriage already contracted. . . . But in the Western Church it is an impediment both to marriage and to the use of marriage."

229. Cf. Deut. 25:5: "When brothers reside together, and one of them dies and has no son, the wife of the deceased shall not be married outside the family to a stranger. Her husband's brother shall go in to her, taking her in marriage, and performing the duty of a husband's brother to her."

by God. Much more should the man here keep faith with his first betrothed, since he could not promise marriage to a second except with a lying heart; and therefore did not really promise it, but deceived her, his neighbor, against God's command. Therefore, the "impediment of error"[227] enters in here, by which his marriage to the second woman is rendered null and void.

The "impediment of ordination" is also the mere invention of men, especially since they prate that it annuls even a marriage already contracted.[228] They constantly exalt their own ordinances above the commands of God. I do not indeed sit in judgment on the present state of the priestly order, but I observe that Paul charges a bishop to be the husband of one wife.[e] Hence, no marriage of deacon, priest, bishop, or any other order can be annulled, although it is true that Paul knew nothing of this species of priests and of the orders we have today. Perish then those cursed human ordinances which have crept into the church only to multiply perils, sins, and evils! There exists, therefore, between a priest and his wife a true and indissoluble marriage, approved by the divine commandment. But what if wicked men in sheer despotism prohibit or annul it? So be it! Let it be wrong among men; it is nevertheless right before God, whose command must take precedence if it conflicts with the commands of men.[f]

An[g] equally lying invention is that "impediment of public decency," by which contracted marriages are annulled. I am incensed at that foolhardy wickedness which is so ready to put asunder what God has joined together that one may well recognize Antichrist in it, for it opposes all that Christ has done and taught. What earthly reason is there for holding that no relative of a deceased fiancé, even to the fourth degree of consanguinity, may marry his fiancée? That is not a judgment of public decency, but ignorance of public decency. Why was not this judgment of public decency found among the people of Israel, who were endowed with the best laws, the laws of God? On the contrary, the next of kin was even compelled by the law of God to marry the widow of his relative.[229] Must the people of Christian lib-

---

e   1 Tim. 3:2.

f   Acts 5:29.

g   The following two paragraphs are not in the Wittenberg and Jena editions; see n. 219, p. 102.

erty be burdened with more severe laws than the people of legal bondage?[230]

But, to make an end of these—figments rather than impediments—I will say that so far there seem to me to be no impediments that may justly annul a contracted marriage except these: sexual impotence, ignorance of a previously contracted marriage, and a vow of chastity. Still, concerning this latter vow, I am to this day so far from certain that I do not know at what age such a vow is to be regarded as binding, as I also said above in discussing the sacrament of baptism. Thus you may learn, from this one question of marriage, how wretchedly and desperately all the activities of the church have been confused, hindered, ensnared, and subjected to danger through pestilent, ignorant, and wicked ordinances of men, so that there is no hope of betterment unless we abolish at one stroke all the laws of all men, and having restored the gospel of liberty we follow it in judging and regulating all things. Amen.

[Impotence]

We must therefore speak of sexual impotence, in order that we may the more readily advise the souls that are laboring in peril. But first I wish to state that what I have said about impediments is intended to apply after a marriage has been contracted. I mean to say that no marriage should be annulled by any such impediment. But as to marriages which are yet to be contracted, I would briefly repeat what I have said above. If there is the stress of youthful passion or some other necessity for which the pope grants dispensation, then any brother may also grant a dispensation to another or even to himself, and following that counsel snatch his wife out of the power of tyrannical laws as best he can. For with what right am I deprived of my liberty by somebody else's superstition and ignorance? If the pope grants a dispensation for money, why should not I, for my soul's salvation, grant a dispensation to myself or to my brother? Does the pope set up laws? Let him set them up for himself, and keep hands off my liberty, or I will take it by stealth!

Now[h] let us discuss the matter of impotence.

230. The "people of legal bondage" (*populum servitutis legalis*) is certainly a pejorative phrase regarding Israel in the Old Testament, but the language is shaped by Pauline usage, especially Galatians 4, rather than another kind of anti-Jewish sentiment.

---

h   The next two paragraphs were left out of the Wittenberg and Jena editions; see n. 231, p. 109.

Consider the following case: A woman, wed to an impotent man, is unable to prove her husband's impotence in court, or perhaps she is unwilling to do so with the Mass of evidence and all the notoriety which the law demands; yet she is desirous of having children or is unable to remain continent. Now suppose I had counseled her to procure a divorce from her husband in order to marry another, satisfied that her own and her husband's conscience and their experience were ample testimony of his impotence; but the husband refused his consent to this. Then I would further counsel her, with the consent of the man (who is not really her husband, but only a dweller under the same roof with her), to have intercourse with another, say her husband's brother, but to keep this marriage secret and to ascribe the children to the so-called putative father. The question is: Is such a woman saved and in a saved state? I answer: Certainly, because in this case an error, ignorance of the man's impotence, impedes the marriage; and the tyranny of the laws permits no divorce. But the woman is free through the divine law, and cannot be compelled to remain continent. Therefore the man ought to concede her right, and give up to somebody else the wife who is his only in outward appearance.

Moreover, if the man will not give his consent, or agree to this separation—rather than allow the woman to burn with desire[i] or to commit adultery—I would counsel her to contract a marriage with another and flee to a distant unknown place. What other counsel can be given to one constantly struggling with the dangers of natural emotions? Now I know that some are troubled by the fact that the children of this secret marriage are not the rightful heirs of their putative father. But if it was done with the consent of the husband, then the children will be the rightful heirs. If, however, it was done without his knowledge or against his will, then let unbiased Christian reason, or better, charity, decide which one of the two has done the greater injury to the other. The wife alienates the inheritance, but the husband has deceived his wife and is defrauding her completely of her body and her life. Is not the sin of a man who wastes his wife's body and life a greater sin than that of the woman who merely alienates the temporal goods of her husband? Let him,

---

i   1 Cor. 7:9.

therefore, agree to a divorce, or else be satisfied with heirs not his own, for by his own fault he deceived an innocent girl and defrauded her both of life and of the full use of her body, besides giving her an almost irresistible cause for committing adultery. Let both be weighed in the same scales. Certainly, by every right, fraud should recoil on the fraudulent, and whoever has done an injury must make it good. What is the difference between such a husband and the man who holds another man's wife captive together with her husband? Is not such a tyrant compelled to support wife and children and husband, or else to set them free? Why should not the same hold true here? Therefore I maintain that the man should be compelled either to submit to a divorce or to support the other man's child as his heir. Doubtless this would be the judgment of charity. In that case, the impotent man, who is not really the husband, should support the heir of his wife in the same spirit in which he would at great expense wait on his wife if she fell sick or suffered some other ill; for it is by his fault and not by his wife's that she suffers this ill. This I have set forth to the best of my ability, for the strengthening of anxious consciences, because my desire is to bring my afflicted brothers and sisters in this captivity what little comfort I can.[231]

[Divorce]

As to divorce, it is still a question for debate whether it is allowable.[j] For my part I so greatly detest divorce that I should prefer bigamy to it;[232] but whether it is allowable, I do not venture to decide. Christ himself, the Chief Shepherd, says in Matt. 5[:32]: "Every one who divorces his wife, except on the ground of unchastity, makes her an adulteress; and whoever marries a divorced woman commits adultery." Christ, then, permits divorce, but only on the ground of unchastity. The pope must, therefore, be in error whenever he grants a divorce for any other cause; and no one should feel safe who has obtained a dispensation by this temerity (not authority) of the pope. Yet it is still a greater wonder to me, why they compel a man to remain unmarried after being separated from his wife by divorce, and why they will not permit him to remarry.[k] For if Christ permits divorce

j   Cf. *Decr. Greg. IX*, lib. 5, tit. 19, *de divortiis.*
k   Cf. *Decr. Greg. IX*, lib. 4, tit. 19, *de divortiis*, c. 2.

231. The advice given here was clearly found to be difficult by Luther's followers who removed it from the edition in his collected works. Still, several factors ought to be considered when judging the two preceding paragraphs: (1) Couched in the language of the scholars only, this Latin treatise was not intended for popular consumption but rather as a guide for bewildered and confused priests, who were called upon in the confessional to give practical advice and spiritual comfort to troubled souls. (2) The impediment of impotency was, even according to Roman church law, sufficient ground for declaring a marriage null and void. (3) But the legal process of securing an annulment demanded such an involved procedure for establishing proof that it was equally unpleasant for both parties. (4) Then, as now, divorce under any circumstances was absolutely forbidden by Roman church law. (5) As an alternate to an impossible legal solution, Luther's suggestion of a secret marriage was not without precedent; common law in parts of Westphalia and Lower Saxony, for example, prescribed that a man who could not perform his conjugal duty was required to seek satisfaction for his wife through a neighbor.

232. Luther famously gave this advice later to King Henry VIII of England and Landgrave Philip of Hesse, regarding it to be the lesser of two evils insofar as it was not without divinely sanctioned precedent in the Old Testament. This phrase, "that I should prefer bigamy to it," was deleted from the Wittenberg and Jena editions; see n. 231.

on the ground of unchastity and compels no one to remain unmarried, and if Paul would rather have us marry than burn with desire,[l] then he certainly seems to permit a man to marry another woman in the place of the one who has been put away. I wish that this subject were fully discussed and made clear and decided, so that counsel might be given in the infinite perils of those who, without any fault of their own, are nowadays compelled to remain unmarried; that is, those whose wives or husbands have run away and deserted them, to come back perhaps after ten years, perhaps never! This matter troubles and distresses me, for there are daily cases, whether by the special malice of Satan or because of our neglect of the Word of God.

I, indeed, who alone against all cannot establish any rule in this matter, would yet greatly desire at least the passage in 1 Cor. 7[:15] to be applied here: "But if the unbelieving partner desires to separate, let it be so; in such a case the brother or sister is not bound." Here the Apostle gives permission to put away the unbeliever who departs and to set the believing spouse free to marry again. Why should not the same hold true when a believer—that is, a believer in name, but in truth as much an unbeliever as the one Paul speaks of—deserts his wife, especially if he intends never to return. I certainly can see no difference between the two. But I believe that if in the Apostle's day an unbelieving deserter had returned and had become a believer or had promised to live again with his believing wife, it would not have been permitted, but he too would have been given the right to marry again. Nevertheless, in these matters I decide nothing (as I have said), although there is nothing that I would rather see decided, since nothing at present more grievously perplexes me, and many others with me. I would have nothing decided here on the mere authority of the pope and the bishops; but if two learned and good men agreed in the name of Christ[m] and published their opinion in the spirit of Christ, I should prefer their judgment even to such councils as are assembled nowadays, famous only for numbers and authority, not for scholarship and saintliness. Therefore I hang up my lyre[233] on this matter until a better man confers with me about it.

233. An allusion to Luther's remarks at the beginning of the treatise that he is writing a "prelude." Cf. Ps. 137:1-2: "By the rivers of Babylon—there we sat down and there we wept when we remembered Zion. On the willows there we hung up our lyres."

l   1 Cor. 7:9.

m   Cf. Matt. 18:19-20.

Ordination

Of this sacrament the church of Christ knows nothing; it is an invention of the church of the pope. Not only is there nowhere any promise of grace attached to it, but there is not a single word said about it in the whole New Testament. Now it is ridiculous to put forth as a sacrament of God something that cannot be proved to have been instituted by God. I do not hold that this rite, which has been observed for so many centuries, should be condemned; but in sacred things I am opposed to the invention of human fictions. And it is not right to give out as divinely instituted what was not divinely instituted, lest we become a laughingstock to our opponents. We ought to see that every article of faith of which we boast is certain, pure, and based on clear passages of Scripture. But we are utterly unable to do that in the case of the sacrament under consideration.

The church has no power to make new divine promises of grace, as some prate, who hold that what is decreed by the church is of no less authority than what is decreed by God, since the church is under the guidance of the Holy Spirit.[234] For the church was born by the word of promise through faith, and by this same word is nourished and preserved. That is to say, it is the promises of God that make the church, and not the church that makes the promise of God. For

This 1561 engraving illustrates one aspect of ordination to the priesthood: the laying on of hands. The bishop stands and lays his hands on the head of each person being ordained. The ordainee kneels and carries a chasuble, a priestly vestment, over one arm.

the Word of God is incomparably superior to the church, and in this Word the church, being a creature, has nothing to decree, ordain, or make, but only to be decreed, ordained, and made. For who begets his own parent? Who first brings forth his own maker?

This one thing indeed the church can do: It can distinguish the Word of God from the words of men; as Augustine confesses that he believed the gospel because he was moved by the authority of the church which proclaimed that this is the

234. Cf. John 14:16-17, 26: "And I will ask the Father, and he will give you another Advocate, to be with you forever. This is the Spirit of truth. But the Advocate, the Holy Spirit, whom the Father will send in my name, will teach you everything, and remind you of all that I have said to you"; John 16:13: "When the Spirit of truth comes, he will guide you into all the truth."

235. Augustine, *Against the Epistle of Manichaeus Called "Fundamental"* 5, 6: "I should not believe the gospel except as moved by the authority of the church catholic."

236. Augustine, *On the Trinity* 9, 6, 10: "the judgment of truth from above is still strong and clear, and rests firmly upon the utterly indestructible rules of its own right; and if it is covered as it were by cloudiness of corporeal images, yet is not wrapped up and confounded in them."

237. Cf. 1 Cor. 2:11-13: "For what human being knows what is truly human except the human spirit that is within? So also no one comprehends what is truly God's except the Spirit of God. Now we have received not the spirit of the world, but the Spirit that is from God, so that we may understand the gifts bestowed on us by God. And we speak of these things in words not taught by human wisdom but taught by the Spirit, interpreting spiritual things to those who are spiritual."

238. Salt was used in connection with the rite of baptism, given to catechumens in the early church to signify purification, wisdom, and the promise of immortality; cf. Augustine, *Confessions* 1, 11. Candles were blessed especially for their use in Candelmas, the Feast of the Purification of Mary. Herbs, fruits, and flowers were often blessed at the beginning of the harvest season in connection with the Feast of the Assumption of Mary.

gospel.[235] Not that the church is therefore above the gospel; if that were true, the church would also be above God, in whom we believe, because it is the church that proclaims God is God. But, as Augustine says elsewhere,[236] the truth itself lays hold on the soul and thus renders it able to judge most certainly of all things; however, the soul is not able to judge the truth, but is compelled to say with unerring certainty that this is the truth. For example, our mind declares with unerring certainty that three and seven are ten; and yet it cannot give a reason why this is true, although it cannot deny that it is true. It is clearly taken captive by the truth; and, rather than judging the truth, it is itself judged by it. There is such a mind also in the church, when under the enlightenment of the Spirit she judges and approves doctrines; she is unable to prove it, and yet is most certain of having it. For as among philosophers no one judges the general concepts, but all are judged by them, so it is among us with the mind of the Spirit, who judges all things and is judged by no one, as the Apostle says.[237] But we will discuss this another time.

Let this then stand fast: The church can give no promises of grace; that is the work of God alone. Therefore she cannot institute a sacrament. But even if she could, it still would not necessarily follow that ordination is a sacrament. For who knows which is the church that has the Spirit? For when such decisions are made there are usually only a few bishops or scholars present; and it is possible that these may not be really of the church. All may err, as councils have repeatedly erred, particularly the Council of Constance,[n] which erred most wickedly of all. Only that which has the approval of the church universal, and not of the Roman church alone, rests on a trustworthy foundation. I therefore admit that ordination is a certain churchly rite, on a par with many others introduced by the church fathers, such as the consecration of vessels, houses, vestments, water, salt, candles, herbs, wine, and the like.[238] No one calls any of these a sacrament, nor is there in them any promise. In the same manner, to anoint a man's hands with oil, or to shave his head and the like is not to administer a sacrament, since no promise is attached to them; they are simply being prepared for a certain office, like a vessel or an instrument.

n   See n. 52, p. 28.

But you will say: "What do you do with Dionysius, who in his *Ecclesiastical Hierarchy* enumerates six sacraments, among which he also includes ordination?"[239] I answer: I am well aware that this is the one writer of antiquity who is cited in support of the seven sacraments, although he omits marriage and so has only six. But we read nothing at all about these "sacraments" in the rest of the fathers; nor do they ever regard them as sacraments when they speak of these things. For the invention of sacraments is of recent date.[240] Indeed, to speak more boldly, it greatly displeases me to assign such importance to this Dionysius, whoever he may have been, for he shows hardly any signs of solid learning. I would ask, by what authority and with what arguments does he prove his hodge-podge about the angels in his *Celestial Hierarchy*—a book over which many curious and superstitious spirits have cudgeled their brains? If one were to read and judge without prejudice, is not everything in it his own fancy and very much like a dream? But in his *Theology*, which is rightly called *Mystical*, of which certain very ignorant theologians make so much, he is downright dangerous, for he is more of a Platonist than a Christian. So if I had my way, no believing soul would give the least attention to these books. So far, indeed, from learning Christ in them, you will lose even what you already know of him. I speak from experience. Let us rather hear Paul, that we may learn Jesus Christ and him crucified.[o] He is the way, the life, and the truth;[p] he is the ladder[q] by which we come to the Father, as he says: "No one comes to the Father, but by me."[r]

Similarly, in the *Ecclesiastical Hierarchy*, what does this Dionysius do but describe certain churchly rites, and amuse himself with allegories without proving anything? Just as has been done in our time by the author of the book entitled *Rationale divinorum*.[241] Such allegorical studies are for idle people. Do you think I should find it difficult to amuse myself with allegories about anything in creation? Did not Bonaventura by allegory draw the liberal arts into theology?[242] And Gerson even converted the smaller Donatus into a mystical theologian.[243] It would not be

o   1 Cor. 2:2.
p   John 14:6.
q   Cf. Gen. 28:12; John 1:51.
r   John 14:6.

239. Dionysius the Areopagite (a pseudonymous author from the sixth century) wrote several influential writings marked by a strong neo-Platonic structure. The *Ecclesiastical Hierarchy* lists as sacraments baptism, the Eucharist, unction, priestly ordination, monastic ordination, and burial.

240. A number of sacraments were listed in early Scholasticism with Peter Lombard's numbering of seven in his *Sentences* (4, d. 2, c. 1) winning general acceptance. These were not made official church doctrine until the bull *Exultate Deo* at the Council of Florence in 1439.

241. Guillaume Durandus (c. 1230–1296), bishop of Mende, wrote an explanation of the rites, ceremonies, and vestments used in the Mass: *Rationale divinorum officiorum* (i.e., "Explanation for the Divine Offices").

242. Like Aquinas, Bonaventure of Bagnoregio (1221–1274) sought to bring correlation and harmony between theological and philosophical knowledge. However, his *Opusculum de reductione artium ad theologiam* (*Little Work on the Restoration of the Arts to Theology*) takes a different approach than Aquinas, seeing the arts and sciences echoing in theology through types and figures.

243. Jean Gerson (1363–1429) was chancellor of the University of Paris. In addition to his influence in ecclesiastical affairs, Gerson also wrote several popular devotional and pastoral works. Luther is referring to his allegory of the *Ars minor*, a Latin grammar written by the fourth-century Roman grammarian, Aelius Donatus (flourished mid-fourth century).

244. Nine statements of Origen were condemned as heretical after his death by an edict of Emperor Justinian I (c. 483–565) and published by the Council of Constantinople in 553; see n. 64, p. 32.

245. The "indelible character" (*character indelibilis*) as a special mark or seal left on the soul after receiving three of the seven sacraments: baptism, confirmation, and ordination. Because the soul has been impressed with this mark, the sacrament cannot be repeated. After ordination a priest, therefore, can never be a layman again. The notion was first officially set forth by the Council of Florence in 1439, "Among these sacraments there are three—baptism, confirmation, and orders—which indelibly impress upon the soul a character, i.e. a certain spiritual mark which distinguishes them from the rest."

difficult for me to compose a better hierarchy than that of Dionysius; for he knew nothing of pope, cardinals, and archbishops, and put the bishop at the top. Who has so weak a mind as not to be able to launch into allegories? I would not have a theologian devote himself to allegories until he has exhausted the legitimate and simple meaning of the Scripture; otherwise his theology will bring him into danger, as Origen discovered.[244]

Therefore a thing does not need to be a sacrament simply because Dionysius so describes it. Otherwise, why not also make a sacrament of the funeral processions, which he describes in his book, and which continue to this day? There will then be as many sacraments as there have been rites and ceremonies multiplied in the church. Standing on so unsteady a foundation, they have nevertheless invented "characters" which they attribute to this sacrament of theirs and which are indelibly impressed on those who are ordained.[245] Whence do such ideas come, I ask? By what authority, with what arguments, are they established? We do not object to their being free to invent, say, and assert whatever they please; but we also insist on our liberty, that they shall not arrogate to themselves the right to turn their opinions into articles of faith, as they have hitherto presumed to do. It is enough that we accommodate ourselves to their rites and ceremonies for the sake of peace; but we refuse to be bound by such things as if they were necessary to salvation, which they are not. Let them lay aside their despotic demand, and we shall yield free obedience to their wishes, in order that we may live in peace with one another. It is a shameful and wicked slavery for a Christian, who is free, to be subject to any but heavenly and divine ordinances.

We come now to their strongest argument. It is this: Christ said at the Last Supper: "Do this in remembrance of me."[s] "Look," they say, "here Christ ordained the apostles to the priesthood." From this passage they also concluded, among other things, that both kinds are to be administered to the priest alone. In fact, they have drawn out of this passage whatever they pleased, as men who would arrogate to themselves the liberty to prove anything whatever from any words of Christ. But is that interpreting the words of God? I ask you: Is it? Christ gives us no promise here, but only commands that this be done in remembrance of

s   Luke 22:19; 1 Cor. 11:24-25.

him. Why do they not conclude that he also ordained priests when he laid upon them the office of the Word and baptism, and said: "Go into all the world and preach the gospel to the whole creation, baptizing them in the name, etc."[t] For it is the proper duty of priests to preach and to baptize. Or, since it is nowadays the chief, and (as they say) indispensable duty of priests to read the canonical hours,[246] why have they not discovered the sacrament of ordination in those passages in which Christ commanded them to pray, as he did in many places—particularly in the garden, that they might not enter into temptation?"[u] But perhaps they will evade this argument by saying that it is not commanded to pray; it is enough to read the canonical hours. Then it follows that this priestly work can be proved nowhere in the Scriptures, and thus their praying priesthood is not of God; as, indeed, it is not.

But which of the ancient fathers claimed that in this passage priests were ordained? Where does this new interpretation come from? I will tell you. They have sought by this means to set up a seedbed of implacable discord, by which clergy and laypersons should be separated from each other farther than heaven from earth, to the incredible injury of the grace of baptism and to the confusion of our fellowship in the gospel. Here, indeed, are the roots of that detestable tyranny of the clergy over the laity.[247] Trusting in the external anointing by which their hands are consecrated, in the tonsure and in vestments, they not only exalt themselves above the rest of the lay Christians, who are only anointed with the Holy Spirit, but regard them almost as dogs and unworthy to be included with themselves in the church. Hence they are bold to demand, to exact, to threaten, to urge, to oppress, as much as they please. In short, the sacrament of ordination has been and still is an admirable device for establishing all the horrible things that have been done hitherto in the church, and are yet to be done. Here Christian brotherhood has perished, here shepherds have been turned into wolves, servants into tyrants, churchmen into worse than worldlings.

If they were forced to grant that all of us that have been baptized are equally priests, as indeed we are, and that only the

246. The canonical hours are the seven daily prayer offices part of the early monastic tradition. Inspired in part by the words of Ps. 119:164, "Seven times a day I praise you for your righteous laws," they are respectively: matins (including nocturns and lauds), prime, tierce, sext, nones, vespers, and compline.

247. Cf. Luther's earlier treatise *The Address to the Christian Nobility* (1520), in which he identifies this spiritual division between the laity and the priesthood as one of the "Roman walls" that the papacy has erected to protect itself from being reformed. It is in this place that Luther introduces the notion that the priesthood in the New Testament has been given to all people through baptism and that ordination only signifies an office that exercises publicly the spiritual authority that all Christians possess. Luther's most thorough articulation of this spiritual priesthood of the baptized was set forth in his subsequent treatise against Hieronymus Emser (see n. 11, p. 14.) *Answer to the Hyperchristian, Hyperspiritual and Hyperlearned Book by Goat Emser in Leipzig* (1521), LW 39:137–224.

t   Mark 16:15; Matt. 28:19.

u   Matt. 26:41.

ministry was committed to them, yet with our common consent, they would then know that they have no right to rule over us except insofar as we freely concede it. For thus it is written in 1 Pet. 2[:9]: "You are a chosen race, a royal priesthood, and a priestly royalty." Therefore we are all priests, as many of us as are Christians. But the priests, as we call them, are ministers chosen from among us. All that they do is done in our name; the priesthood is nothing but a ministry. This we learn from 1 Cor. 4[:1]: "This is how one should regard us, as servants of Christ and stewards of the mysteries of God."

From this it follows that whoever does not preach the Word, though he was called by the church to do this very thing, is no priest at all, and that the sacrament of ordination can be nothing else than a certain rite by which the church chooses its preachers. For this is the way a priest is defined in Mal. 2[:7]: "The lips of a priest should guard knowledge, and people should seek instruction from his mouth, for he is the messenger of the Lᴏʀᴅ of hosts." You may be certain, then, that whoever is not a messenger of the Lord of hosts, or whoever is called to do anything else than such messenger service—if I may so term it[248]—is in no sense a priest; as Hos. 4[:6] says: "Because you have rejected knowledge, I reject you from being a priest to me." They are also called shepherds[v] because they are to shepherd, that is, to teach. Therefore, those who are ordained only to read the canonical hours and to offer Masses are indeed papal priests, but not Christian priests, because they not only do not preach, but they are not even called to preach. Indeed, it comes to this, that a priesthood of that sort is a different estate altogether from the office of preaching. Thus they are hour-reading and Mass-saying priests—sort of living idols called priests—really such priests as Jeroboam ordained, in Beth-aven, taken from the lowest dregs of the people, and not of Levi's tribe.[w]

See how far the glory of the church has departed! The whole earth is filled with priests, bishops, cardinals, and clergy; yet not one of them preaches so far as his official duty is concerned, unless he is called to do so by a different call over and above his sacramental ordination. Every one thinks he is doing full justice to his ordination by mumbling the vain repetitions of his

248. Luther is playing with the broader and narrower meanings of *angelus domini* in Malachi 2, i.e., messenger and angel.

v   Lat. *pastores.*

w   1 Kgs. 12:31.

prescribed prayers and by celebrating Masses. Moreover, he never really prays when he repeats those hours; or if he does pray, he prays them for himself. And he offers his Mass as if it were a sacrifice, which is the height of perversity because the Mass consists in the use made of the sacrament. It is clear, therefore, that the ordination, which, as a sacrament, makes clergymen of this sort of men, is in truth nothing but a mere fiction, devised by men who understand nothing about the church, the priesthood, the ministry of the Word, or the sacraments. Thus, as the "sacrament" is, so are the priests it makes. To such errors and such blindness has been added a still worse captivity: in order to separate themselves still farther from other Christians, whom they deem profane, they have emasculated themselves, like the Galli, who were the priests of Cybele,[249] and they have taken upon themselves the burden of a spurious celibacy.

To satisfy this hypocrisy and the working of this error it was not enough that bigamy should be prohibited, that is, the having of two wives at one time, as it was forbidden in the law (and as is the accepted meaning of the term); but they have called it bigamy if a man marries two virgins, one after the other, or if he marries one widow.[250] Indeed, so holy is the holiness of this most holy sacrament that no man can become a priest if he has married a virgin and his wife is still living.[x] And—here we reach the very summit of sanctity—a man is even prevented from entering the priesthood if he has married a woman who was not a virgin, though he did so in ignorance or by unfortunate mischance.[251] But if one has defiled six hundred harlots, or violated countless matrons and virgins, or even kept many Ganymedes,[252] that would be no impediment to his becoming bishop or cardinal or pope. Moreover, the Apostle's word "husband of one wife" [1 Tim. 3:2] must now be interpreted to mean "the prelate of one church," and this has given rise to the "incompatible benefices."[253] At the same time the pope, that munificent dispenser, may join to one man three, twenty, or a hundred wives, that is, churches, if he is bribed with money or power, that is, "moved by godly charity and constrained by the care of the churches."[y]

O pontiffs worthy of this venerable sacrament of ordination! O princes, not of the catholic churches, but of the synagogues of

x   Cf. *Decr. Greg. IX*, lib. 1, tit. 21, *de bigamis non ordinandis*, c. 3.
y   2 Cor. 11:28.

249. Galli (sg. Gallus) was the name for the eunuch priests who served Cybele, the ancient Phrygian goddess of nature whose worship became part of the cultic practices in the Roman Empire.

250. Aquinas, *STh* III Suppl., q. 66, a. 1: "By the sacrament of order a man is appointed to the ministry of the sacraments; and he who has to administer the sacraments to others must suffer from no defect in the sacraments. . . . the perfect signification of the sacrament requires the husband to have only one wife, and the wife to have but one husband; and consequently bigamy, which does away with this, causes irregularity. And there are four kinds of bigamy: the first is when a man has several lawful wives successively; the second is when a man has several wives at once, one in law, the other in fact; the third, when he has several successively, one in law, the other in fact; the fourth, when a man marries a widow."

251. Aquinas, *STh* III Suppl., q. 66, a. 3: "Gregory says, 'We command thee never to make unlawful ordinations, nor to admit to holy orders a bigamist, or one who has married a woman that is not a virgin, or one who is unlettered, or one who is deformed in his limbs, or bound to do penance or to perform some civil duty, or who is in any state of subjection.'"

252. In Greek mythology, Ganymede was the youthful consort of Zeus.

253. Benefices, rents, and profits derived from lands endowed to the church (see the earlier note on the church and feudal system, p. 73) in exchange for spiritual services were part of the livelihood for bishops. Laws were originally enacted that prevented bishops from holding more than one benefice, but the distinction between "compatible" and "incompatible" benefices was used to justify plurality in a variety of cases, as sanctioned by the pope. This distinction was used toward widespread abuse and was part of the reforms taken up by the Council of Trent.

Satan[z] and of darkness itself! I would cry out with Isaiah, "You scoffers, who rule this people in Jerusalem";[a] and with Amos 6[:1], "Woe to those who are at ease in Zion, and to those who feel secure on the mountain of Samaria, the notable men of the first of the nations, that go in with state into the house of Israel, etc.!" O the disgrace that these monstrous priests bring upon the church of God! Where are there any bishops or priests who even know the gospel, not to speak of preaching it? Why then do they boast of being priests? Why do they desire to be regarded as holier and better and mightier than other Christians, who are merely laymen? To read the hours—what unlearned men, or (as the Apostle says) men speaking with tongues[b] cannot do that? But to pray the hours—that belongs to monks, hermits, and men in private life, even though they are laymen. The duty of a priest is to preach, and if he does not preach he is as much a priest as a picture of a man is a man. Does ordaining such babbling priests make one a bishop? Or blessing churches and bells? Or confirming children? Certainly not. Any deacon or layman could do as much. It is the ministry of the Word that makes the priest and the bishop.

Therefore my advice is: Begone, all of you that would live in safety; flee, young men, and do not enter upon this holy estate, unless you are determined to preach the gospel, and can believe that you are made not one whit better than the laity through this "sacrament" of ordination! For to read the hours is nothing, and to offer Mass is to receive the sacrament. What then is there left to you that every layperson does not have? Tonsure and vestments? A sorry priest, indeed, who consists of tonsure and vestments! Or the oil poured on your fingers? But every Christian is anointed and sanctified both in body and soul with the oil of the Holy Spirit. In ancient times every Christian handled the sacrament with his hands as often as the priests do now. But today our superstition counts it a great crime if the laity touch either the bare chalice or the corporal;[254] not even a nun who is a pure virgin would be permitted to wash the palls and the sacred linens of the altar. O God! See how far the sacrosanct sanctity of this "sacrament" of ordination has gone! I expect the time will

254. The "corporal" is the altar cloth upon which the consecrated bread and wine are placed.

z   Rev. 2:9.

a   Isa. 28:14

b   Cf. 1 Cor. 14:23.

come when the laity will not be permitted to touch the altar—except when they offer their money. I almost burst with indignation when I contemplate the wicked tyrannies of these brazen men, who with their farcical and childish fancies mock and overthrow the liberty and glory of the Christian religion.

Let all, therefore, who know themselves to be Christian, be assured of this, that we are all equally priests, that is to say, we have the same power in respect to the Word and the sacraments. However, no one may make use of this power except by the consent of the community or by the call of a superior. (For what is the common property of all, no individual may arrogate to himself, unless he is called.) And therefore this "sacrament" of ordination, if it is anything at all, is nothing else than a certain rite whereby one is called to the ministry of the church. Furthermore, the priesthood is properly nothing but the ministry of the Word—the Word, I say; not the law, but the gospel. And the diaconate is the ministry, not of reading the Gospel or the Epistle, as is the present practice, but of distributing the church's aid to the poor, so that the priests may be relieved of the burden of temporal matters and may give themselves more freely to prayer and the Word. For this was the purpose of the institution of the diaconate, as we read in Acts 5.[255] Whoever, therefore, does not know or preach the gospel is not only no priest or bishop, but he is a kind of pest to the church, who under the false title of priest or bishop, or dressed in sheep's clothing, actually does violence to the gospel and plays the wolf[256] in the church.

Therefore, unless these priests and bishops, with whom the church abounds today, work out their salvation[c] in some other way; unless they realize that they are not priests or bishops, and bemoan the fact that they bear the name of an office whose duties they either do not know or cannot fulfill, and thus with prayers and tears lament their wretched hypocritical life—unless they do this, they are truly the people of eternal perdition, and the words of Isa. 5[:13f.] are fulfilled in them: "Therefore my people go into exile for want of knowledge; their nobles are dying of hunger, and their multitude is parched with thirst. Therefore, Hell has enlarged its appetite and opened its mouth beyond measure, and the nobility of Jerusalem and her multitude go down, her throng

255. Luther is referring to the setting apart of Stephen and six others to distribute food to the poor and widows in Acts 6:1-4.

256. Cf. Matt. 7:15: "Beware of false prophets, who come to you in sheep's clothing but inwardly are ravenous wolves."

c   Cf. Phil. 2:12.

and he who exults in her." What a dreadful word for our age, in which Christians are swallowed up in so deep an abyss!

According to what the Scriptures teach us, what we call the priesthood is a ministry. So I cannot understand at all why one who has once been made a priest cannot again become a layperson;[257] for the sole difference between him and a layperson is his ministry. But to depose a man from the priesthood is by no means impossible, because even now it is the usual penalty imposed upon guilty priests. They are either suspended temporarily, or permanently deprived of their office. For that fiction of an "indelible character" has long since become a laughingstock. I admit that the pope imparts this "character," but Christ knows nothing of it; and a priest who is consecrated with it becomes the lifelong servant and captive, not of Christ, but of the pope, as is the case nowadays. Moreover, unless I am greatly mistaken, if this sacrament and this fiction ever fall to the ground, the papacy with its "characters" will scarcely survive. Then our joyous liberty will be restored to us; we shall realize that we are all equal by every right. Having cast off the yoke of tyranny, we shall know that the one who is a Christian has Christ; and that the one who has Christ has all things that are Christ's, and can do all things.[d] Of this I will write more,[258] and more vigorously, as soon as I perceive that the above has displeased my friends the papists.

The Sacrament of Extreme Unction

To this rite of anointing the sick the theologians of our day have made two additions that are worthy of them: first, they call it a sacrament, and second, they make it the last sacrament. So it is now the sacrament of extreme unction, which is to be administered only to those who are at the point of death. Since they are such subtle dialecticians,[e] perhaps they have done this in order to relate it to the first unction of baptism and the two subsequent ones of confirmation and ordination.[259] But here they are able to cast in my teeth that, in the case of this sacrament, there are on the authority of the apostle James both promise

257. Because of the notion of indelible character; see n. 245, p. 114.

258. Luther takes this up in his subsequent treatise, *The Freedom of the Christian* (1520), LW 31:327–77; TAL 1:466–538.

259. Cf. Lombard, *Sentences* 4, d. 23, c. 2: "And there are three kinds of anointing. For there is an anointing which is done with chrism [i.e., confirmation], which is called the principal anointing . . . there is also another anointing by which catechumens and neophytes are anointed on the breast and between the shoulders at the reception of baptism. But there is a third anointing which is called the oil of the sick."

d   Cf. Phil. 4:13.
e   See n. 25, p. 17.

and sign, which, as I have maintained all along, do constitute a sacrament. For the apostle says [Jas. 5:14-15]: "Are any among you sick? They should call for the elders of the church and have them pray over them, anointing them with oil in the name of the Lord. The prayer of faith will save the sick, and the Lord will raise them up; and anyone who has committed sins will be forgiven." There, they say, you have the promise of the forgiveness of sins and the sign of the oil.

But I say: If ever folly has been uttered, it has been uttered especially on this subject: I will say nothing of the fact that many assert with much probability that this epistle is not by James the apostle, and that it is not worthy of an apostolic spirit;[260] although, whoever was its author, it has come to be regarded as authoritative. But even if the apostle James did write it, I still would say, that no apostle has the right on his own authority to institute a sacrament, that is, to give a divine promise with a sign attached. For this belongs to Christ alone. Thus Paul says that he received from the Lord the sacrament of the Eucharist,[f] and that he was not sent to baptize, but to preach the gospel.[g]

This detail of the *Seven Sacraments* altarpiece by artist Roger van der Weyden (c. 1400–1464) shows the sacrament of extreme unction.

And nowhere do we read in the gospel about the sacrament of extreme unction. But let us also pass over the point. Let us examine the words of the apostle, or whoever was the author of the epistle, and we shall see at once how little heed these multipliers of sacraments have given to them.

In the first place, if they believe the apostle's words to be true and binding, by what right do they change and contradict them? Why do they make an extreme and a special kind of unction out

f   1 Cor. 11:23.
g   1 Cor. 1:17.

260. The apostolicity and authorship of the epistle of James were long debated in the church. For example, Jerome regarded the text as pseudonymous, and Eusebius, in his *Church History*, numbers it among the New Testament texts whose authority had been contested, i.e., *antilegomena*. In Luther's day, Erasmus questioned its authorship, and Luther's Wittenberg colleague Andreas von Karlstadt published a treatise (*De canonicis scripturis*

libellus) only a few months earlier that gave a detailed treatment of the question of James's authority and place in the canon.

261. Lombard takes up the question of a more general repetition of the sacrament of unction in *Sentences* 4, d. 23, c. 4.

262. For example, the Supplement to Aquinas's *Summa* discusses the fact that the *Ecclesiastical Hierarchy* does not mention extreme unction as one of the sacraments; *STh* III Suppl., q. 29, a. 1.

263. The concluding prayer of the rite of extreme unction, used since the eighth century, included the following: "In your mercy restore him inwardly and outwardly to full health, so that, having recovered through the help of your mercy, he may return to his former duties."

264. E.g., *Exultate Deo*, from the Council of Florence (1439), "this sacrament ought not to be given except to the sick of whom death is feared."

of that which the apostle wished to be general?[261] For the apostle did not desire it to be an extreme unction or administered only to the dying, but he says expressly: "Is any one sick?" He does not say: "Is any one dying?" I do not care what learned discussions Dionysius has on this point in his *Ecclesiastical Hierarchy*.[262] The apostle's words are clear enough, on which he as well as they rely; but they do not follow them. It is evident, therefore, that they have arbitrarily and without any authority made a sacrament and an extreme unction out of the words of the apostle which they have wrongly interpreted. And this works to the detriment of all other sick persons, whom they have deprived on their own authority of the benefit of the unction that the apostle enjoined.

But this is even a finer point: The apostle's promise expressly declares: "The prayer of faith will save the sick, and the Lord will raise them up, etc."[h] See, the apostle in this passage commands us to anoint and to pray, in order that the sick may be healed and raised up; that is, that they may not die, and that it may not be an extreme unction. This is proved also by the prayers that are used even to this day during the anointing, because the prayers are for the recovery of the sick.[263] But they say, on the contrary, that the unction must be administered to none but the dying;[264] that is, that they may not be healed and raised up. If it were not so serious a matter, who could help laughing at this beautiful, apt, and sensible exposition of the apostle's words? Is not the folly of the sophists here shown in its true colors? Because here, as in so many other places, it affirms what the Scriptures deny, and denies what the Scriptures affirm. Why should we not give thanks to these excellent masters of ours? Surely I spoke the truth when I said that they never uttered greater folly than on this subject.

Furthermore, if this unction is a sacrament, it must necessarily be (as they say)[i] an "effective sign" of that which it signifies and promises. Now it promises health and recovery to the sick, as the words plainly say: "The prayer of faith will save the sick, and the Lord will raise them up."[j] But who does not see that this promise is seldom, if ever, fulfilled? Scarcely one in a thousand is

---

h   James 5:15.

i   See nn. 163 and 164, p. 67.

j   James 5:15.

restored to health, and when one is restored nobody believes that it came about through the sacrament, but through the working of nature or of medicine. Indeed to the sacrament they ascribe the opposite effect. What shall we say then? Either the apostle lies in making this promise or else this unction is no sacrament. For the sacramental promise is certain; but this promise fails in the majority of cases. Indeed—and here again we recognize the shrewdness and foresight of these theologians—for this very reason they would have it to be extreme unction, that the promise should not stand; in other words, that the sacrament should be no sacrament. For if it is extreme unction, it does not heal, but gives way to the disease; but if it heals, it cannot be extreme unction. Thus, by the interpretation of these masters, James is shown to have contradicted himself, and to have instituted a sacrament in order not to institute one; for they must have an extreme unction just to make untrue what the apostle intends, namely, the healing of the sick by it. If this is not madness, I ask you what is?

The word of the apostle in 1 Tim. 1[:7] describes these people: "Desiring to be teachers of the law, without understanding either what they are saying or the things about which they make assertions." Thus they read and follow everything uncritically. With the same carelessness they have also found auricular confession in the apostle's words: "Confess your sins to one another."[k] But they do not observe the command of the apostle, that the elders of the church be called, and prayer be made for the sick.[l] Scarcely one insignificant priest is sent nowadays, although the apostle would have many present, not because of the unction, but because of the prayer. That is why he says: "The prayer of faith will save the sick man, etc."[m] I have my doubts, however, whether he would have us understand "priests" when he says "presbyters," that is, "elders." For one who is an elder is not necessarily a priest or a minister. We may suspect that the apostle desired the older, graver men in the church to visit the sick, to perform a work of mercy, and pray in faith and thus heal him. Yet, it cannot be denied that the churches were once ruled by older persons,

k   James 5:16.
l   James 5:14.
m   James 5:15.

chosen for this purpose without these ordinations and consecrations, solely on account of their age and long experience.

Therefore I take it that this unction is the same as that practiced by the apostles, of whom it is written in Mark 6[:13]: "They anointed with oil many that were sick and healed them." It was a rite of the early church, by which they worked miracles on the sick, and which has long since ceased. In the same way Christ, in the last chapter of Mark, gave to believers the power to pick up serpents, lay hands on the sick, etc.[n] It is a wonder that they have not made sacraments of those words also, for they have the same power and promise as these words of James. Therefore this extreme—which is to say fictitious—unction is not a sacrament, but a counsel of James, which anyone who will may follow; and it is derived from Mark 6[:13], as I have said. I do not believe that it was a counsel given to all sick persons, for the church's infirmity is her glory and death is gain;[o] but it was given only to such as might bear their sickness impatiently and with little faith, those whom the Lord allowed to remain in order that miracles and the power of faith might be manifest in them.

James made careful and diligent provision in this case by attaching the promise of healing and the forgiveness of sins not to the unction, but to the prayer of faith. For he says: "And the prayer of faith will save the sick, and the Lord will raise them up; and if anyone has committed sins, they will be forgiven."[p] A sacrament does not demand prayer and faith on the part of the minister, since even a wicked person may baptize and consecrate without prayer; a sacrament depends solely on the promise and institution of God, and requires faith on the part of the recipient. But where is the prayer of faith in our present use of extreme unction? Who prays over the sick one in such faith as not to doubt that he will recover? Such a prayer of faith James here describes, of which he said at the beginning of his epistle: "But ask in faith, with no doubting."[q] And Christ says of it: "Whatever you ask in prayer, believe that you receive it, and you will."[r]

There is no doubt at all that, even if today such a prayer were made over a sick person, that is, made in full faith by older,

---

n   Mark 16:18.
o   Cf. Phil. 1:21.
p   James 5:15.
q   James 1:6.

graver, and saintly men, as many as we wished would be healed. For what could not faith do? But we neglect this faith that the authority of the apostle demands above all else. Further, by "presbyters"—that is, men preeminent by reason of their age and faith—we understand the common herd of priests. Moreover, we turn the daily or temporally unrestricted unction into an extreme unction. And finally, we do not obtain the result promised by the apostle, namely, the healing of the sick, but we render the promise ineffective by doing the very opposite. And yet we boast that our sacrament, or rather figment, is established and proved by this saying of the apostle, which is diametrically opposed to it.[265] O what theologians!

Now I do not condemn this our "sacrament" of extreme unction, but I firmly deny that it is what the apostle James prescribes; for his unction agrees with ours neither in form, use, power, nor purpose. Nevertheless, we shall number it among those "sacraments" which we have instituted, such as the blessing and sprinkling of salt and water. For we cannot deny that any creature whatsoever may be consecrated by the Word and by prayer, as the apostle Paul teaches us.[s] We do not deny, therefore, that forgiveness and peace are granted through extreme unction; not because it is a sacrament divinely instituted, but because he who receives it believes that these blessings are granted to him. For the faith of the recipient does not err, however much the minister may err. For one who baptizes or absolves in jest,[266] that is, one who does not absolve so far as the minister is concerned, nevertheless does truly baptize and absolve if the person to be baptized or absolved believes. How much more will one who administers extreme unction confer peace, even though he does not really confer peace so far as his ministry is concerned, since there is no sacrament there! The faith of the one anointed receives even that which the minister either could not give or did not intend to give. It is sufficient for the one anointed to hear and believe the Word. For whatever we believe we shall receive, that we really do receive, no matter what the minister may or may not do, or whether he dissembles or jests. The saying of Christ holds good: "All things are possible to him who believes,"[t] and again: "Be it done for you

265. Luther uses a Greek proverbial expression here, *dis dia pason*, which signifies a great difference. In music, it was the greatest span in a given scale. Cf. Erasmus, *Adagia* 1, 2, 63.

266. On the Scholastic debate over this question, see, for example, Lombard, *Sentences* 4, d. 6, c. 5, "Concerning One Who Is Immersed in Jest." See also n. 161, p. 66.

r   Mark 11:24.
s   1 Tim. 4:4-5.
t   Mark 9:32.

as you have believed."[u] But in treating the sacraments our sophists say nothing at all of this faith, but only babble with all their might about the virtues of the sacraments themselves.[v] They will "listen to anybody and can never arrive at a knowledge of the truth."[w]

Still it was a good thing that this unction was made the extreme or "last" unction, for thanks to that, it has been abused and distorted least of all the sacraments by tyranny and greed. This one last mercy, to be sure, has been left to the dying—they may be anointed without charge, even without confession and communion.[267] If it had remained a practice of daily occurrence, especially if it had cured the sick, even without taking away sins, how many worlds, do you think, would not the pontiffs have under their control today? For through the one sacrament of penance and the power of the keys, as well as through the sacrament of ordination, they have become such mighty emperors and princes. But now it is a fortunate thing that they despise the prayer of faith, and therefore do not heal any sick, and that they have made for themselves, out of an ancient ceremony, a brand-new sacrament.

Let this now suffice for these four sacraments. I know how it will displease those who believe that the number and use of the sacraments are to be learned not from the sacred Scriptures, but from the Roman See. As if the Roman See had given these "sacraments" and had not rather received them from the lecture halls of the universities, to which it is unquestionably indebted for whatever it has. The papal despotism would not have attained its present position, had it not taken over so many things from the universities. For there was scarcely another of the celebrated bishoprics that had so few learned pontiffs as Rome. Only by violence, intrigue, and superstition has she till now prevailed over the rest. For the men who occupied the See a thousand years ago differed so vastly from those who have since come into power, that one is compelled to refuse the name of Roman pontiff to one group or the other.

267. Luther is speaking of what was regarded as a widespread abuse of the sacrament, in which confession and communion were absent from the administration of extreme unction.

---

u   Matt. 8:13.

v   Cf., for example, Aquinas, *STh* III, q. 69, a. 6.

w   2 Tim. 3:7.

[Other Sacraments]

There are still a few other things which it might seem possible to regard as sacraments; namely, all those things to which a divine promise has been given, such as prayer, the Word, and the cross. For Christ has promised, in many places, that those who pray should be heard; especially in Luke 11,[x] where by many parables he invites us to pray. Of the Word he says: "Blessed are those who hear the Word of God and keep it."[y] And who can count all the times God promises aid and glory to those who are afflicted, suffer, and are cast down? Indeed, who can recount all the promises of God? Why, the whole Scripture is concerned with provoking us to faith; now driving us with commands and threats, now drawing us with promises and consolations. In fact, everything in Scripture is either a command or a promise. The commands humble the proud with their demands; the promises exalt the humble with their forgiveness.

Nevertheless, it has seemed proper to restrict the name of sacrament to those promises which have signs attached to them. The remainder, not being bound to signs, are bare promises. Hence there are, strictly speaking, but two sacraments in the church of God—baptism and the bread.[z] For only in these two do we find both the divinely instituted sign and the promise of forgiveness of sins. The sacrament of penance, which I added to these two, lacks the divinely instituted visible sign, and is, as I have said, nothing but a way and a return to baptism. Nor can the scholastics say that their definition fits penance, for they too ascribe to the true sacrament a visible sign, which is to impress upon the senses the form of that which it effects invisibly.[a] But penance or absolution has no such sign. Therefore they are compelled by their own definition either to admit that penance is not a sacrament and thus to reduce their number, or else to bring forth another definition of a sacrament.

Baptism, however, which we have applied to the whole of life, will truly be a sufficient substitute for all the sacraments that we might need as long as we live. And the bread is truly the

x   Luke 11:5-13.

y   Luke 11:28.

z   Cf. Luther's earlier remarks in which he initially proposes three sacraments; see p. 62, above.

a   Cf. Lombard, *Sentences* 4, d. 1, c. 2.

sacrament of the dying and departing; for in it we commemorate the passing of Christ out of this world, that we may imitate him. Thus we may apportion these two sacraments as follows: baptism may be allotted to the beginning and the entire course of life, while the bread belongs to the end and to death. And the Christian should use them both as long as he is in this mortal frame, until, fully baptized and strengthened, he passes out of this world, and is born into the new eternal life, to eat with Christ in the kingdom of his Father, as he promised at the Last Supper, when he said: "Truly, I say to you, I shall not drink again of this fruit of the vine until it is fulfilled in the kingdom of God."[b] Thus he clearly seems to have instituted the sacrament of the bread with a view to our entrance into the life to come. For then, when the purpose of both sacraments is fulfilled, baptism and bread will cease.

[Conclusion]

Herewith I conclude this prelude, and freely and gladly offer it to all pious souls who desire to know the genuine sense of the Scriptures and the proper use of the sacraments. For it is a gift of no mean importance, to know the gifts that are given to us, as it is said in 1 Cor. 2[:12], and what use we ought to make of them. For if we are instructed with this judgment of the spirit, we shall not mistakenly rely on those things which are wrong. These two things our theologians never taught us; indeed, they seem to have taken pains to hide them from us. If I have not taught them, I certainly managed not to conceal them, and have given occasion to others to think out something better. It has at least been my endeavor to set them both forth. Nevertheless, "not all can do all things."[268] To the godless, on the other hand, and those who in obstinate tyranny force on us their own teachings instead of God's, I confidently and freely oppose these pages. I shall be completely indifferent to their senseless fury. Yet I wish even them a right understanding. And I do not despise their efforts; I only distinguish them from what is sound and truly Christian.

268. Luther is quoting Virgil, *Eclogues* 8, 63.

b   Cf. Matt. 26:29; Mark 14:25; Luke 22:18.

I hear a rumor that new bulls[c] and papal maledictions are being prepared against me, in which I am urged to recant or be declared a heretic.[269] If that is true, I desire this little book to be part of the recantation that I shall make; so that the arrogant despots might not complain of having acted in vain. The remainder I will publish very soon;[270] please Christ, it will be such as the Roman See has never seen or heard before. I shall give ample proof of my obedience. In the name of our Lord Jesus Christ. Amen.

> "Why doth that impious Herod fear
> When told that Christ the King is near?
> He takes not earthly realms away,
> Who gives the realms that ne'er decay."[271]

269. The bull *Exsurge domine*, issued on 15 June 1520, gave Luther and his followers sixty days to recant before they would be declared of heresy. On 10 December, sixty days later, Luther and his colleagues invited the students of Wittenberg to a burning of papal and Scholastic books. There Luther publicly burned *Exsurge domine*. On 3 January 1521, the pope issued the bull *Decet Romanum pontificem*, formally excommunicating Luther.

270. On 29 November 1520, Luther published *Assertion of All the Articles Wrongly Condemned in the Roman Bull*. His treatise *On the Freedom of the Christian* was also published in the same month, with an accompanying letter to Pope Leo X (see LW 31:327-77; TAL 1:466-538).

271. The eighth stanza of Coelius Sedulius's *A solis ortus cardine* (fifth century). Luther would later translate stanzas 8, 9, 11, and 13 as an Epiphany hymn, *Was fürchtst du Feind, Herodes, sehr.*

c   See n. 179, p. 79.

Image Credits

60, 95, 97, 111: Courtesy of the Digital Image Archive, Pitts Theology Library, Candler School of Theology, Emory University.

CPSIA information can be obtained
at www.ICGtesting.com
Printed in the USA
JSHW050427220621
16118JS00002B/45